FOOTBALL FEVER 2

COLLECTED BY
TONY BRADMAN

ILLUSTRATED BY JON RILEY

CORGI BOOKS

FOOTBALL FEVER 2
A CORGI BOOK : 0 552 545279

First publication in Great Britain

PRINTING HISTORY
Corgi edition published 1998

Collection © 1998 by Tony Bradman
Illustrations © 1998 by Jon Riley

'Coming Home' © 1998 by Rob Childs
'Flash' © 1998 by Nick Warburton
'Dan, Dan, the Half-Time Man' © 1998 by Janet Burchett and Sara Vogler
'Tina' © 1998 by Neil Arksey
'Winning by Numbers' © 1998 by Dennis Whelehan
'Haven't You Forgotten Something?' © 1998 by Dennis Hamley
'Shoot-Out' © 1998 by Paul Stewart
'The B Team' © 1998 by Narinder Dhami
'Preston North End' © 1998 by Brian Morse
'The Spider King' © 1998 by Jonathan Kebbe

The right of Tony Bradman to be identified as the Compiler
of this work has been asserted in accordance with
the Copyright, Designs and Patents Act 1988

Set in Bembo by Falcon Oast Graphic Art

Corgi Books are published by Transworld Publishers Ltd,
61–63 Uxbridge Road, Ealing, London W5 5SA,
in Australia by Transworld Publishers (Australia) Pty. Ltd,
15–25 Helles Avenue, Moorebank, NSW 2170,
and in New Zealand by Transworld Publishers (NZ) Ltd,
3 William Pickering Drive, Albany, Auckland.
Made and printed in Great Britain by
Cox & Wyman Ltd, Reading, Berks.

THE SQUAD

Duane jinked round the last player, the goalie came out at him and he chipped the ball over his head. A lovely, delicate shot it was — just over the goalie's outstretched hands and just beneath the bar. One–nil . . .

That's just one of the terrific matchplay moments in this action-packed collection of top-scoring football stories.

With stories from a team of top authors, including Rob Childs, Brian Morse and Paul Stewart, this is the second in a series of football story collections brought to you by Tony Bradman. The first collection, *Football Fever*, is already available from Corgi Books.

Also available from Tony Bradman,
and published by Corgi Books:

FOOTBALL FEVER

AMAZING ADVENTURE STORIES

FANTASTIC SPACE STORIES

INCREDIBLY CREEPY STORIES

GOOD SPORTS: A BAG OF SPORTS
STORIES

A STACK OF STORY POEMS

COMING HOME
by Rob Childs

'*And here's Josh Peters, pouncing on the ball like a panther . . .*'

Josh trod on the football and almost fell over.

'*. . . Peters dribbles his way skilfully towards goal . . .*'

Josh knocked the ball too far and had to fetch it out of the shrubs.

'*. . . The star striker glances up and sees the keeper off his line . . .*'

The garden gnome, acting as goalkeeper, gave the impression it would rather be fishing. Its bent rod dangled sadly in the wet grass.

'*. . . Peters tries a cheeky lob. He must score. Oh! Unlucky!*'

Josh had scooped his shot over the gnome, but over the crossbar too. The ball disappeared into the tall conifers screening the bungalow from the bottom of the long garden. He scowled at the plastic gnome, which at least had the sense to be looking the other way.

'Nice goal.'

Josh whirled round, startled at the sound of another voice cutting across his wild commentary. A boy with tousled fair hair was leaning over the fence, grinning. He seemed strangely familiar.

'No need to be sarcastic. I know my shot was rubbish.'

'I was only admiring the goal. Proper net an' all. Present, was it?'

Josh nodded. 'This Christmas.'

'Must feel great when you smash the ball into the net.'

'Wouldn't know too much about that,' Josh admitted. 'You saw what my shooting's like.'

The boys smiled at each other in understanding, quietly sharing the joke. Josh was surprised not to feel too embarrassed. 'How long have you been standing there?'

'Long enough to know that commentator of yours ought to get the sack!'

'Hoped you might not have heard me.'

'Don't worry. Everybody rants on like that sometimes when they think nobody else's around.'

'Anyone with you?'

'Nope. Just strolling along this footpath, minding my own business – till I saw you here.'

Josh went up to the fence and looked along the path that skirted the open fields behind the gardens. 'Not tried it yet. We've only just moved in. Where does it go to?'

'Up to the recky. And it's a good short cut to school.'

'I'm starting there after the holidays,' Josh sighed. 'Do you play for the school team?'

The boy shook his head. 'Used to. I don't live here any more.'

'Pity. Haven't got to know anyone yet. Do you fancy a game?'

'Thought you'd never ask,' he said, leaping eagerly over the wall. 'As long as I can go in goal first. That's my favourite position.'

'Sure. What's your name? Mine's . . .'

'Josh Peters.'

'How did you know that?'

'I guessed it was probably the only thing the commentator got right!' he laughed. 'My mates call me Dolly.'

'Why Dolly?'

'After my surname,' he replied, retrieving the ball. 'And I'd let poor old Fred go back to the pond, if I were you. We don't need him now.'

'Fred?'

'Yeah, Fred the fisherman!'

'What was all that noise down the garden this afternoon?' asked Mum at tea-time.

'Just me and Dolly playing football,' grinned Josh.

'Odd name for a boy.'

'Don't know his real one. He's coming round again tomorrow.'

Mum caught his dad's eye across the table in relief.

They had both loved this bungalow on the edge of town from the moment they'd first seen it. Their main worry about moving, however, had been whether Josh would settle down at a new school. He didn't tend to find it easy to make friends.

'Useful footballer is he, this Dilly?' said Dad encouragingly.

'Dolly,' Josh corrected him. 'He's dead good in goal. He's going to teach me how to play there. Says that might be my best chance of making the team.'

'Doesn't he play in goal for them?'

'No, he's not at Wexford School now.'

'Where does he go then?' asked Mum out of interest.

'Dunno. He never said.'

'Is he older than you?' she persisted.

Josh shrugged. 'About the same, I guess.'

'Where does he live?'

Again the shrug as Josh put down his knife and fork.

'Sounds a bit of a mystery man, your Dolly,' Dad laughed. 'No doubt you had more important things to talk about. Like how to score goals, eh?'

'And stop 'em,' added Josh.

'I'm pleased you've found someone to play with, anyway, whoever he is,' said Mum. 'We know you were sorry to leave the village, Josh, but there was just something about this place. We simply had to buy it.'

Josh got up from the table. 'I'm glad you did now,' he assured them. 'It's funny. Already feels like I've lived here all my life.'

4

★

Dolly was waiting by the fence when Josh appeared round the conifers the next day.

'You must be freezing in that T-shirt. You should have come and rung the bell instead of shivering to death outside.'

'I'm OK, no need to worry about me.'

'Better not let Mum see you dressed like that,' Josh laughed. 'She'd have you wrapped up in jumpers and scarf straightaway!'

Dolly suddenly looked worried. 'What have you told her about me?'

'Nothing. I don't know anything, do I?'

'Best to keep it like that,' Dolly said pointedly. 'Look, I'm just here to play football, right? I don't want to start getting invited in for tea.'

They enjoyed a good session together. Dolly began in goal again, but this time only to show Josh how to deal with different kinds of shots – when the shooter managed to get them on target.

'I'll never get picked to play for Wexford,' Josh groaned as yet another effort ballooned over the bar. 'The school's massive. They must have loads of kids to choose from.'

'Yeah, but they're lacking a decent keeper this season. Let's see what you're like between the posts.'

They swapped over and Josh's handling at first was not much better than his kicking. He fumbled several of Dolly's low drives, letting one slip over the line through his legs.

'That'll teach you to get your body behind your hands,' Dolly told him with a chuckle. 'Nothing worse than letting a daft goal in like that. I know, I've done it myself in a match. My mates never let me forget it.'

Dolly continued to make coaching points as they practised, helping Josh to gain in confidence with some good stops. The budding keeper felt his best save was when he dived to deflect a well-struck volley round the post. He lay there for a moment on the grass, as if posing for the photographers behind the goal.

Dolly grinned at him. 'Yeah, not bad, but what would happen now in a real game?'

Josh shrugged. 'Well, it'd be a corner.'

'Right, and they might go and score from that corner. Could you have caught the ball, d'yer reckon?'

'Maybe, I guess.'

Dolly nodded. 'Then you could have sent Wexford on the attack instead. Try and hang on to the ball if you can. Keep possession.'

Josh realized the advice was good. 'I'm going to need a lot more practice to get as good as you, Dolly.'

'You're doing fine. We'll make a keeper of you yet,' he promised. 'And a good goalie needs to kick well, too. I'll show you my special drop-kicks tomorrow. I was famous for them. They go miles.'

Dolly's next shot from near the fence sailed wide, however, and Josh jogged off to the conifers just as Mum appeared.

'I came to see if you two boys wanted any hot drinks,'

6

she began and then faltered. 'Oh, I thought Dolly was here with you.'

Josh turned round, but there was no-one to be seen. Dolly had suddenly disappeared.

Mrs Bennett, their elderly neighbour, spoke to Josh's mum later that evening. 'I just had to come and ask,' she began, flustered. 'Who was that boy your Josh was playing with today in the garden?'

Mrs Peters had to smile. 'So there *was* somebody with him. He's called Dolly, apparently. I'm sorry if they were disturbing you.'

'No, no, it's quite all right, I just saw them from my kitchen window.'

'I'm glad to hear it. When he was little, you see, Josh went through a phase of having an imaginary friend – like some children do,' Mrs Peters explained. 'He was so real to Josh, though, we even had to put out an extra place at the meal table for this invisible Christopher sometimes. I was almost afraid he'd come back again!'

Mrs Bennett still looked pale. 'Sorry to bother you,' she apologized. 'My old eyes must be playing tricks on me. The other boy just reminded me of somebody, that's all. Very silly. Couldn't have been him of course.'

Mrs Peters was puzzled. 'Why do you say that?'

'Sorry, doesn't matter now. Forgive me,' the old lady murmured, starting to back away. 'Long time ago. Please forget I ever mentioned it. Must go and get on with things.'

'Now what was that all about, I wonder?' Josh's mum said to herself as Mrs Bennett shuffled quickly away up the drive.

The following afternoon, Josh had a similar question of his own when he met up with Dolly again. 'Why did you go and scarper like that yesterday?' he demanded. 'You made me look a fool.'

Dolly skipped nimbly over the fence, still wearing the same blue T-shirt and tracksuit bottoms as before. He made no response.

'C'mon, where did you shoot off to so quick? I reckon Mum thought I'd gone mad – or was making you up. Or both!'

Dolly shrugged. 'Sorry. Saw your mum heading our way.'

'So? What have you got against meeting parents?'

'Nothing. They just tend to ask too many questions.'

Josh took the hint and shut up. The session was devoted to kicking practice. His dead-ball kicks were fine, but he found the drop-kicks out of his hands harder to do properly. Josh watched open-mouthed when his friend demonstrated the art. The ball was struck perfectly on the half-volley and sent whirling away into the field.

'Wow! How did you do that?' Josh gasped, knowing Dolly wouldn't mind answering that kind of question.

'Skill,' Dolly grinned. 'But it does need something else too.'

'What's that?'

'A ball. Go and fetch!'

Josh trudged back into the field half-a-dozen times after close study of Dolly's technique. He watched how the goalie balanced himself as he tossed the ball up and then made firm contact with his left instep the instant it hit the ground.

'Good job we're both left-footed. Makes it easier for me to try and copy your action.'

'See how the ball stays real low,' Dolly said with pride. 'Specially useful when you're playing into a strong wind. Ordinary high kicks can get blown back at you, but these fly further than the other team expects. Catches them out.'

'Why don't we go and practise on the recky?' Josh suggested. 'There might be a few other kids there. Save a lot of chasing about.'

'Nah! Stay here. Don't want everybody learning my secret. I'm doing this just for your benefit, you know.'

Josh felt quite privileged. And anyway, he reasoned, he'd be doing the kicking now and making Dolly do most of the running.

It didn't quite work like that. Josh's early efforts were comical. The first he missed altogether, the second smashed into the low fence and the third was sliced into the bushes.

'This is trickier than it looks,' he grunted.

Josh concentrated fiercely on his next kick and this time managed to connect better. He launched the ball over Dolly's head, over the fence and out into the middle of the field.

'Right, good,' grinned his coach. 'Just need to get the timing right. You'll get the hang of it with practice.'

It took lots of practice. The boys met up every afternoon that week to keep working on Josh's handling and kicking skills – even when it rained on the final day of the Christmas holidays.

'Mum thinks I'm crazy wanting to play outside today,' Josh said. 'But I knew you'd be here.'

'Surprised she's not come sneaking down to spy on us,' said Dolly.

'Told her not to. But she won't let me stay out too long in this weather.'

'Better than nothing. It lets me give you one last work-out.'

'Last one?' cried Josh in dismay. 'Have you got to go?'

' 'Fraid so. I've taught you all I know,' Dolly said with a rueful smile. 'Reckon now you'll be able to show 'em at the school they've got a good new keeper. Bet old Simpo will soon spot you.'

'Simpo?'

'Yeah, Mr Simpson. He runs the school team. Been here for yonks, but he's OK. They usually win something every season.'

'Wish me luck. Fingers crossed.'

'You can't save shots with your fingers crossed,' Dolly grinned.

It was several days before the footballers at the school took much notice of the new boy in Mr Simpson's class.

He didn't look as though he was any good when he nervously joined in the lunchtime kickabouts in the playground – until the time Josh took a turn between the coats.

He was tested out immediately. Ryan, Wexford's team captain, blasted the ball at goal and was already turning to celebrate as Josh got his body behind the swerving shot and hugged it safely to his chest.

He smiled to himself, pleased to overhear some grudging praise from the other players. After two more saves, Ryan strolled up to him. 'Josh, is it?' he asked casually. 'You play in goal for your last school?'

Josh decided to bluff it out. 'Yeah, mostly.'

Ryan seemed satisfied with the answer. 'Why don't you come to our practice after school tomorrow? Simpo's always moaning about us letting in too many goals.'

That was music to his ears. Tomorrow, as far as Josh was concerned, could not come soon enough.

When it finally did, Mr Simpson put Josh through his paces straightaway – and liked what he saw. He had lads smacking shots at the newcomer from all angles and was impressed by Josh's clean handling and positioning.

'Ryan told me about your goalkeeping,' the teacher said to him with a smile. 'And he was right too. Welcome to the Wexford soccer squad!'

Josh's confidence soared. In the practice match that followed, he felt as though he had always been a goal-keeper. He made it look that way as well. He hit top form in the big goals, letting very few shots or crosses escape his clutches. He remembered Dolly's advice – hold on to the ball.

As Dolly flashed into his mind, something made him glance over towards the hedge at the far side of the large playing fields. He thought he spotted his special pal next to one of the trees, but danger threatened his goal and he had to concentrate on the game. When he checked again moments later, there was no-one in sight.

Mr Simpson stroked his chin thoughtfully as he watched Josh in action. 'It's uncanny,' he said to himself. 'The way he goes down for a ball, the way he catches it. His style is just like . . . No, that's stupid.'

The teacher tried to put the image out of his mind, but it was no use – especially after he saw the goalkeeper do a drop-kick clearance. In the fading winter light, Josh struck the ball sweetly on the half-volley, left-footed, sending the ball snaking upfield well over the halfway line.

'Fantastic!' whooped Ryan. 'Never seen a kick like that before.'

'I have,' murmured Mr Simpson under his breath. 'Ten years ago . . .'

He whistled the game to a halt. 'Well done, lads, I think we can look forward to a bit more success this term.' He paused and winked at Josh. 'Maybe we'll give our new signing his debut in goal in the Cup next Saturday, eh?'

When Mr Simpson joined them in the cloakroom

later, he was carrying a framed photograph. 'Glad to see you're still here, Josh,' he said. 'I wanted to show you this. Just went to get it from the staffroom.'

The players grouped around the teacher to peer at the picture of a team of young footballers. Two rows of boys in smart red kit posed for the camera, with a younger-looking Mr Simpson standing proudly at the side. In front of them gleamed two trophies.

'Just look at those weird haircuts!' Ryan giggled.

'You'll earn the right to mock, captain, if your team does half as well as this one,' chuckled the teacher. 'Best squad of players I've ever had at this school. They won the League and Cup Double without losing a game.'

'We won the Cup last season,' Ryan reminded him. 'But I think it's a different shape to those two trophies.'

'You're right. We started up a new competition the year after this photo was taken.' He paused for a moment, struck by a coincidence. 'It'd be about the time you people were born, I suppose ...'

Mr Simpson broke off again. 'Are you feeling OK, Josh?'

The others turned towards him. 'You've gone dead white,' said Ryan. 'You look like you've just seen a ghost!'

The colour had drained from Josh's face. 'Who . . . who's the goalie?' he croaked, pointing to the fair-haired boy in the green top who was grinning out from the back row of the picture.

'Strange you should ask that,' said Mr Simpson. 'The goalie is the lad I wanted to talk to *you* about. You remind me of him, you see, the way you keep goal. Where did you learn drop-kicks like that?'

Josh didn't know what to say, even if he could have found his voice. It would have been difficult to tell the truth at the best of times, that he'd only just been taught how to do them. But he was still trying to recover from the shock of seeing his personal coach in the old team photograph. All he could do was shake his head.

The teacher regarded him carefully before continuing. 'And even stranger, Josh, is the fact that this lad used to live where you do now. In the very same bungalow. I went there to see him when he became ill. Before he died.'

'Died?' Josh felt himself go cold. 'Dolly?'

'Yes. Although I called him Chris. You obviously know of him, then. Not related at all, are you, by any chance?'

Josh shook his head again. It was beginning to swim and he sat down heavily on a bench, feeling dizzy. Nothing made sense.

'Chris caught meningitis and died in the summer holidays,' Mr Simpson explained sadly to the footballers. 'A terrible tragedy. He was a smashing lad and an excellent goalkeeper. The local schools named a new Cup in his honour.'

'Is that the won we won?' asked Ryan.

The teacher nodded. 'It's called the Christopher Dolman Memorial Trophy. Be nice to win it again this season, too, eh?' He caught Josh's eye and gave him a reassuring smile. 'Especially for Dolly . . .'

FLASH
by Nick Warburton

It was a good, tight game. Nil–nil for seventy minutes and not many chances at either end. Then Duane got the ball out on the left, just inside our half, and went on one of his weaves. That's what he calls these runs he does from time to time: weaves. He wove his way past three of their defenders, cut inside and held the ball up, just a little. Jason went tearing outside him, pulling one of the full-backs wide. Then Duane jinked round the last player, the goalie came out at him and he chipped the ball over his head. A lovely, delicate shot, it was – just over the goalie's outstretched hands and just beneath the bar. One–nil. Which is the way it stayed. That piece of skill was the difference between the sides.

Duane is our most skilful player by a mile. He's what Mr Stubbs calls a match-winner.

Mr Stubbs ran on the pitch at the final whistle, grabbed hold of Duane and swung him round.

'A piece of pure skill, Flash,' he said. 'Ten seconds of magic.'

Then he said to the rest of us, 'Well played, lads. Nice performance.'

He said it over his shoulder as we walked in, and you could tell that he thought Duane was the real star. Which was fair enough because he was. Like I said, he's a considerable player. The best. You can't help noticing him.

He's also my twin brother.

They call Duane 'Flash' for obvious reasons. They call me Clyde because Clyde is my name. You don't get called a special name if you never do anything special. I played at right full-back and I did what I had to do. Made some interceptions. Put in some tackles, a few long clearances. No-one would call it magic.

We trooped off to get changed.

'Great goal, Duaney,' the lads said, flocking round. 'Goal of the month. No question.'

'Till the next game,' laughed Duane.

He wasn't exactly cocky with it, but he knew he was good and he didn't mind talking about it. He also knew how to make the other kids laugh. Back in the changing rooms he re-ran the goal for us, playing all the parts himself. One moment he was Duane, weaving his way upfield, and the next he was the goalie, desperately clawing at the air. Then he was the crowd, waving its arms

17

and cheering. Everyone fell about. Even I had to smile. A bit.

There wasn't really much of a crowd. It was a school game on the school field. Mr Stubbs was there, of course, and a few mums and dads. And Mr Bywater, the school caretaker. Mr Bywater always watched our games if he could. He was a bit of a player himself in the old days, so he said. He'd tell you about it if you had the time to stand around and listen. The other kids didn't really bother any more. They'd heard Mr Bywater's stories before, and they tended to drift off when he started with the memories. I was about the only one who gave him time.

As we left the changing rooms, he was still plodding up and down the corridor with his broom. A bit like a cart-horse. It was hard to think of him dashing about a pitch with muscly legs and shiny hair.

'Nice game, boys,' he said. 'Good win.'

'See Duaney's goal, did you, Mr B?' said Jason.

'Course I did. Lovely bit of skill. Reminds me of one I scored myself. When I played in the Church league. We were up against the leaders. A point behind with two games to play . . .'

'Yeah,' said Jason. 'You told us before.'

And off they went. Mr Bywater leaned on his broom a moment, remembering. Then he noticed me.

'Well played, Clyde,' he said. 'You got through a lot of donkey work out there.'

Donkey work, I thought, stuffing my boots in my bag.

That's what I am. A donkey. Duane's a magician and I'm a donkey.

On the way home, Duane was still full of it. I walked in a dead straight line and he was nipping about and waving his arms and yacking non-stop. Every now and again he'd grin at me, big and broad, and I'd give him a little smile back.

After a while he said, 'You're very quiet, Clyde.'

'I'm always quiet.'

'Today you're quieter. So what is it? You didn't enjoy the game?'

'The game was fine,' I said.

'Then what's wrong?'

I walked along with my eyes fixed on the pavement for a while. Then I said, 'You see what I did in the game, Duane?'

'You did all right, Clyde. You did all right.'

'But did you see — actually see — what I did?'

'Well . . .'

'No, you didn't. Because nobody did. I didn't get noticed.'

'Of course you got noticed . . .'

'So what did I do? You can't say, can you? And that's what's up, Duane. You're brilliant and I'm not. I know I shouldn't mind, but I do.'

He stopped skipping about and walked beside me for a while. 'I've been going on about my goal, haven't I?' he said.

'A bit.'

'I'm sorry, Clyde. You should've told me to shut it.'

'No,' I said. 'It's not your fault you're the magician and I'm the donkey.'

'No. Rubbish. I'm just flash, that's all. I shout my mouth off about it.'

He had no more to say after that, but he rested his hand on my shoulder as we walked along. When we got in, he told Dad all about the game. 'And you should've seen Clyde,' he said, helping himself to bread and jam. 'The way he slid across the goalmouth to clear off the line. Spectacular. I thought we were done for.'

He's all right, Duane is. He may be a bit mouthy, but he's all right. Dad looked at me over the top of his glasses. 'Really?' he said. 'You did that, Clyde? Well done.'

And I just smiled in a modest kind of way, as if to say, 'It was nothing much really.'

Which was true. It wasn't anything much. Duane had made it up.

That night I was lying in bed thinking things over when I heard Duane's voice drift down from the top bunk.

'Clyde,' he said. 'You awake?'

'Hmm.'

'I've been thinking.'

'What about?'

'I'm a bit of a show-off, right?'

'Yes.'

20

'No, you don't have to pretend. I know I am. It's just the way I am. Flash.'

'So?'

'So I get noticed. And I've been thinking that that's what you've got to do, Clyde. Be a bit more flash.'

'Me? But . . .'

'No, I've been thinking and it's the only answer. Get noticed, man. Be a bit more flash.'

Flash? Me? It didn't seem right somehow. But I drifted off to sleep thinking about it.

Well, I slept on it and dreamed a bit about it, and when I woke up the next morning, I'd more or less made my mind up. I'd give it a go. So after breakfast I made sure everyone else was busy and I took a ball into the garden for a bit of practice. I tried flipping the ball on the end of my toe, then over my head and spinning round to smash it against the shed wall on the volley. The first time I tried I missed completely and nearly wrenched my leg off. A couple of times later I managed to connect but the ball sliced off my foot and ballooned over the fence where it smacked against Mrs Craven's washing.

'I saw that! I saw what you just did!' came a voice from an upstairs window.

'Sorry, Mrs Craven,' I said, nipping through the fence. 'It sort of slipped.'

'You'll sort of slip if I get hold of you. You and your fancy footwork.'

'I'll be a bit more careful next time.'

'It's football, football all the time with you, Duane. Why can't you take up stamp-collecting or something?'

I couldn't help smiling as I scrambled back into our garden. She thought I was Duane. I must've been doing something right, then.

I kept up the practice, before and after school, all week, always making sure that no-one else was around. The way I saw it, the new, improved Clyde with the added ingredient – flash – was a secret weapon, and you don't show off your secret weapon until you're good and ready.

We had our next game on Saturday morning against St David's and I didn't have to wait long to demonstrate my new-found skills. We'd already played St David's three times – a friendly, a league match and in the Cup – so they knew us quite well. After about five minutes, a long ball came down their left wing and I went out to meet it. It wasn't too much of a problem. Their number eleven was haring after it, his elbows pumping and his cheeks puffing, but I was favourite to get there first. Normally I would've hoofed it upfield or killed it and sent it sideways to one of our centre-backs. Nice and safe and steady. No fuss and no flash. But that was the old Clyde. This time I had other plans.

I trapped the ball and dribbled it towards the on-coming winger. Then I swerved towards the touchline, and, when he changed direction and came after me, I stepped over the ball and back-heeled it to Carl, our centre-back. The winger wasn't expecting such amazing flair and slipped over as he tried to slam into reverse. Which made me feel great. Unfortunately, Carl wasn't expecting it either. His eyes were fixed on their penalty area where he thought the ball was about to land.

'Behind you, Carl! Behind you!' bellowed Mr Stubbs from the touchline.

Carl doubled back and collected the ball just before their striker pounced on it, so the danger passed. It looked a bit naff, but I reckoned that wasn't my fault. Carl should've kept his wits about him.

Just before half-time, there was a scramble in our area and I managed to collect the ball a yard or two off the goal line. Two St David's players came at me from the left and the right and for a moment it looked like there'd be a Clyde sandwich followed by a goal, but I put my toe on the ball, dummied one way, flicked it the other, side-stepped and began to bring it clear.

'Get rid of it! Get rid of it!' shouted Mr Stubbs.

But I wasn't finished yet and I didn't get rid of it. I buzzed round the penalty area like a wasp, looking round for Duane. At that moment, just as I looked up, I saw this blur of a St David's shirt and suddenly the ball was no longer at my feet. I heard a thump and when I turned round, our goalie was on his hands and knees and the ball was bobbling about in the back of the net.

We managed to scrape a draw. I don't need to tell you who got the equalizer.

'Soft goal,' hissed Mr Stubbs afterwards. 'A real soft goal. We just gave it to them on a plate.'

Of course, by 'we' he meant me. He didn't say so, but then he didn't have to. I knew it was my fault, and I could tell the others thought so too by the way they wouldn't look at me. Even Duane looked away when I caught his eye. I don't think he meant anything by it. He was just embarrassed and didn't know what to say.

The only one who said anything at all to me was Mr Bywater.

'You were looking very confident out there today,' he said.

'Yeah.'

'Trying something new, if I'm not mistaken.'

Yeah, I thought. Giving away goals.

The following Tuesday the team for the next game – the last of the season – was posted on the noticeboard and I wasn't in it.

'This isn't fair,' said Duane as we stood in the corridor staring at it.

'Of course it is,' I said. 'I gave away a soft goal and now I have to pay for it.'

'Look, you made a mistake, Clyde. One mistake.'

'One mistake's enough,' I said and walked away.

'Don't give up, though,' he called after me. 'You just need a bit more practice, that's all.'

Thursday evenings we played five-a-side in the school hall and Mr Stubbs sat around watching and taking notes. It wasn't really a training session; we just played for the fun of it. For a couple of days I was feeling so low I thought I'd give it a miss. I wasn't in the team any more so why should I bother to turn up? But, like Duane said, you don't just give up, do you? So I turned up with the others.

This particular Thursday we didn't get started straightaway. Mr Bywater was still sweeping the hall and we had to wait till he'd finished.

'Give us a couple of moments, lads,' he called out as he marched up and down with his broom. 'I've had chairs to stack all afternoon and I'm all behind.'

So we sat on the stage and watched him for a couple of moments. And a couple of moments more. Mr Bywater was always very thorough and he liked his hall floors perfect.

'Come on,' Carl said eventually. 'We're not eating off it; we're playing football on it.'

And he jumped down and dribbled the ball into the path of Mr Bywater's broom.

'Hey! Let me do a decent job, Carl, please!'

Then the others swarmed on too, and began to run rings round him.

'There're spots of dinner still on this floor,' grumbled Mr Bywater. 'I have to finish the job properly . . .'

But the game got under way around him and there was nothing he could do about it. He retired to the side of the hall, muttering under his breath. I wasn't in the first game so I sat next to him for a while.

'You have to let a bloke do a decent job,' he said. 'It's

very important to me, a decent job.'

I smiled and nodded. Actually, I thought he was just making a fuss, but as it turned out, he was right. It *was* important to do a proper job.

'Look at that, Clyde,' he said a moment later, pointing to the middle of the hall.

'What?'

'There's a pea I've overlooked. An overlooked pea. It isn't right.'

Before I could make out the offending pea, Carl had found it with his heel. His eyes and mouth were wide as he skidded into a pile of P.E. mats. For a second there was silence, then everyone was running over to see if he was all right.

'Me ankle,' he moaned. 'I've done me ankle in.'

'How did this come about?' asked Mr Stubbs, kneeling by him and waving the others out of the way.

'Don't know. I put me foot down and it just went. Skid.'

Mr Bywater looked at me and pulled a face. 'What did I say? One solitary pea, and it brings a lad down. I said, didn't I? Let me do a proper job.'

Carl could hardly put any weight on his ankle. He's in the same boat as I am, I thought. He'll miss our last game. But he wasn't. It didn't occur to me at first, but after the incident with the overlooked pea, we were a man short. Mr Stubbs shook his head and looked round the hall at the rest of us.

'Nothing else for it,' he said. 'Clyde'll have to take his place.'

He made it sound like a real nuisance. Nothing else for it. We have to lose a decent player and put a donkey in instead. It didn't do much for my confidence, but when I realized I was back in the team, I was determined to make the most of it. Carl's bad luck had given me another chance, a chance to show Mr Stubbs that he was wrong not to want me. By the final whistle on Saturday he'd change his mind. I'd make sure he would.

Just before kick-off I was sitting on the ground pulling twists of grass from my studs and trying not to think too much about the game. I always get a bit nervous before a match, but it was a lot worse today.

'How're you feeling?' said a voice above me.

I looked up and saw Mr Bywater silhouetted against a watery sun.

'I'm OK,' I said.

He squatted down beside me and lowered his voice. 'I've got something for you,' he said, pulling a small cardboard box from his jacket pocket. 'A good-luck charm.'

He set the box on the grass beside me and waited for me to open it, like uncles do at Christmas, keeping one eye on you and the other on the present.

'You shouldn't, Mr B,' I began as I pulled the lid off.

There in a nest of cotton wool was a small green object, a bit like a marble. I couldn't work it out.

'It looks like a pea,' I said, blinking up at him.

'That's because it is a pea,' he said.

'But. . . what for?'

I didn't intend to sound ungrateful, but, I mean, a pea?

'It was a pea that gave you this chance, Clyde. This isn't the same one, of course. That's just a small green skid mark. This is what you might call a substitute. Even so it's a bit special.'

'Is it?'

'It's like you and me, that pea. Overlooked. You and me have a job to do, Clyde, but nobody seems to notice.'

I know it sounds daft – a wrinkled pea in a box – but I suddenly felt quite choked. I thanked him, tucked the little box in my tracksuit pocket and headed for the pitch.

'One more thing, Clyde,' he called after me. I turned round and looked at him. 'A pea on a hall floor,' he said quietly, 'is not where a pea ought to be. Every thing and every person has his place and his purpose.' He paused and frowned for a moment, as if he wasn't sure I'd understand him. 'You can read a game, Clyde,' he went on. 'You know where to be and when to be there. It's what you're good at. And you make it look simple. Not many lads can do that. Don't try to be what you're not. You know what I mean?'

Across the pitch Duane was going on one of his practice weaves and jabbering away at the others at the same time. Mr Stubbs was clapping his hands and shouting encouragement from the touchline.

'That's the way, Flash! Show us what you can do!'

'Yes,' I said to Mr Bywater. 'I think I know what you mean.'

29

'Get out there and play, then,' he said. 'Your game, no-one else's.'

We won that last game – two–nil. No-one had much to say about my performance but I didn't really mind. I knew what I'd done. After the match, Mr Stubbs called us together and presented Duane with a medal he'd had engraved: Player of the Year. It was no surprise to the rest of us but it thrilled Duane. He propped it on the mantel-piece at home.

Pride of place, next to a little cardboard box with a green pea in it.

DAN, DAN THE HALF-TIME MAN
by Janet Burchett and Sara Vogler

'That Dan – he's so slow a tortoise could tackle him.'

'And he'd be so long getting out of the changing room he'd meet the team coming back.'

'Yeah, and if he did a circuit of the pitch he'd have to take his pyjamas.'

Dan Craddock tried to shrink down in his seat at the back of the school bus – which was hard for a boy who was as round as the oranges he handed out at half-time. Dan was the largest and most devoted fan of West Oldfield Road Sunday Team. Chaz Patel, their manager, had appointed him team caterer and physiotherapist. It was a posh name for the boy who cuts up oranges and splashes wet sponges about. Football was Dan's life. He would have given anything to be in the team, even if it was only as Harry the Substitute's substitute. And then maybe one magnificent day . . .

'. . . *And it's Craddock. He receives a good ball. He hits it strongly . . . and knocks it in! That's his hat trick. They've only been on the pitch four minutes . . .*'

As the commentator's voice faded, Dan could still hear Sidney Trump and his mate broadcasting his skills to the whole bus. Blaring it out like the loudspeaker at Wembley.

Dan listened to the sniggers. No-one was shouting about Sid and his only attempt at goal last Sunday. No-one was shouting about the ball hitting the woodwork and bouncing straight back to Sid's feet. Sid had been so busy celebrating his near miss he didn't notice it.

'Even I could have scored from there,' thought Dan.

Still, he was entitled to wear the West Oldfield Road Sunday Team sweatshirt. He wore it with pride. Sadly, no-one had realized what the initials spelt until the shirts came back from the printers: WORST FC. And they were. They were the worst in the Sunday league. They were so bad their dads didn't even bother to fight on the touch-line any more. For as long as anyone could remember they'd come fifteenth. There were fifteen teams in the league.

That Sunday, Dan chopped oranges into neat wedges.

'What a waste of time,' he thought. 'Oranges don't make goals. We haven't scored for fifty-eight matches.'

Chaz was giving his pre-match talk. 'I want my team to play total football. I want us to play a passing game,

balls to feet. And Tracy – boots on the right feet this
week. Let's be getting up into their penalty area . . .'

Dan looked round the motley crew that were the
team. They had trouble getting up in the morning.

'. . . I want the defence to move out as one and that's
down to you, Gita. If they play the offside game, we do
the same. I want total commitment from everybody. And
don't pick your nose on the pitch, Vince.'

The team looked about as lively as a row of last year's
turnips. They didn't believe they could win any more.
Dan was worried they were going to break up and
where would that leave him? He wasn't even good
enough for a free transfer. An orange squirted in his eye.
He couldn't see the point in having oranges. All the
players did was have a quick slurp and toss them to the
ground. What a way to treat his little segments.

Then an idea kicked off in his brain and ran up the
wing. Play began, but he was so busy thinking that he
didn't see Gita's clumsy tackle that gave the other side a
penalty. He was so busy thinking, he didn't notice Jim
the Goalie tread on his own boot-laces as he tried to save
the penalty. He was so busy thinking, he barely heard
Sid's vicious comments as he lumbered on to the pitch
with his plate at half-time. He'd got it! The idea bounced
twice round his skull and hit the back of the net. He
couldn't wait to get home.

Everyone was out so he had the kitchen to himself. He
was going to concoct something. Something to wake

them up. Something to make them win.

He experimented all afternoon. He liked the colour of the lemon and mustard drink but felt it might be a touch too lively. The jam and tomato sauce tasted OK but Jim the Goalie always fainted at the sight of blood. Especially as it was usually his.

'If I can get this right,' thought Dan, 'it might even work on me.' He pictured the scene.

'. . . . *And it's Craddock. What a run this boy has made. Craddock on his left foot, still Craddock. He's leaving the defenders standing. He won't shoot from there, will he? No . . . Yes, he has! My word, what a goal! This boy is destined for the premiership . . .'*

Dan came back to earth with a burp. He was feeling sick. He couldn't bring himself to try the cayenne pepper and sprout purée – it might cause some explosive runs. In the end, apple juice and marmalade were the only jars he hadn't opened. It could work. He'd try it on the team next Sunday.

'What's this?' snarled Sid. 'Where's me orange? Footballers always have oranges.'

'It's apple juice with a hint of marmalade.'

'Don't like the bits in marmalade,' said Gita.

'It'll give you energy for the second half,' said Dan, encouragingly.

Jim the Goalie had a taste. 'This is good,' he said. 'The bitterness of the peel contrasting subtly with the sweet autumnal flavours of the apple.'

The others risked a sip. They had seconds. Sid had thirds.

The team seemed unusually lively as they ran out for the second half.

Dan wondered if his drink was working already. WORST FC kicked off. Gita took the ball up the wing. She crossed to Sid who, for a change, saw the ball coming and was in the right position. It was a great pass.

'It must be the drink,' thought Dan. 'We don't usually keep possession for more than thirty seconds.'

The opposition were not prepared for this – WORST FC on the attack! Sid had plenty of room. He drilled the ball into the back of the net.

WORST FC's seven supporters were too stunned to cheer. Chaz Patel stood gobsmacked.

'It's working!' yelled Dan.

It took the referee some time to disentangle the players from their celebratory scrum.

Then WORST FC were on the attack again! Gita passed to Vince. Vince on towards Sid. Sid ran with the ball. It could be another goal. He was about to shoot when suddenly he crumpled. He crossed his legs and groaned with pain. The referee blew his whistle.

'I never touched him,' yelled the big defender.

Dan ran on with his sponge. Chaz and Harry the Substitute were close behind.

'I'm not hurt,' panted Sid. 'I'm just busting!'

He winced off to the loo. Tracy followed, then Gita,

then Jim the Goalie. Five minutes later there were only three of their team left on the pitch – and they looked pale.

WORST FC lost eleven–one.

'We should have stuck to oranges,' hissed Sid.

But Dan knew it would work – if he got the formula right. After all, they'd scored a goal. Something less liquidy was called for. He flicked through his recipe book. Rock cakes? Sausage rolls? Toffee . . . ? Toffee! Made with skimmed milk. It would be energizing but not heavy – and at least they'd stick on the pitch.

Next Sunday they were three down at half-time. The team groaned when they saw Dan's plate of toffees.

'I want me orange,' moaned Sid.

'Now, team,' said Chaz. 'That was a first half that simmered rather than boiled. Remember last week. Remember the goal. Forget what happened after. Focus on that goal. Let's keep right bang up there. Anyone need the loo?' Without thinking he took a toffee. 'Mmmmn,' he grinned.

Jim the Goalie had a lick. 'It's energizing but there's no hint of the heaviness you normally associate with toffee.' He started chewing.

They all had one.

They were still chewing when the second half started. Finchley Avenue Sunday Team swept out from defence.

'Markammmm!' yelled Jim the Goalie.

Chaz tried to shout instructions from the bench. 'Brghmh!' he garbled. 'Lookagoogoo!'

The striker dodged round Vince, who was attempting to force his jaws apart. He whizzed past Gita, who had her finger stuck to a tooth. Jim the Goalie was too busy getting toffee out of his molars with his goalkeeper gloves. *Smack!* The ball hit the back of the net.

They lost thirteen–nil.

When Chaz finally removed the toffee from his teeth, he didn't have the heart to blame Dan.

'We were always in the game,' he said.

Sid tripped Dan up as he went past.

Desperate, Dan decided to have one last go for their home match against Trafford Old Place FC next Sunday. Then he'd go back to the oranges. One last attempt to find something refreshing without bladder problems. Taste without lockjaw. Something that was light and invigorating. He looked in his recipe book.

On Sunday, Trafford Old Place were two–nil up at half–time.

Dan pulled back the tea towel to reveal his fluffy white creations.

'Not again,' snarled Sid.

Chaz looked nervous. He'd been at the dentist for three hours on Monday.

'You first,' said Gita to Tracy.

'After you,' said Vince to Harry the Substitute.

Jim the Goalie took a mini-meringue. He stared at it long and hard and then shoved it quickly in his mouth. The others watched anxiously as he chewed. 'Delicious,' he said. 'It's airy with a refreshing liquid centre. Orange and honey, I believe. Light and invigorating.'

As Jim the Goalie could still speak, the others fell upon the mini-meringues. They even squabbled over the last one before racing on to the pitch for the second half.

Jim the Goalie had a system. He would dive to the right three times and then to the left three times, unless it was a leap year. Occasionally he connected with the ball. Today he got it right. He saw the striker bearing down on him. He dived to the left and the ball slammed into his belly. As he creased up in pain he found his arms clutching the ball. It was an amazing save.

'The boy done brilliant!' gasped Chaz. 'I can't bear to watch.'

And he didn't. Dan and Harry the Substitute commentated for him. It was an exciting second half. Jim the Goalie's save, or the meringues, or something had turned it into a different ball game.

'Tracy's got the ball now,' said Dan. 'That's a good touch to Sid.'

'He's gone wide,' continued Harry the Substitute. 'He's crossed it. No, it was too deep.'

'But Gita's picked it up. She's breaking out to the right. She's ridden a tackle – and she's gone for goal . . .'

Chaz peeped through his fingers.

'She's beaten the goalie,' shrieked Dan. 'Ohhh! She's been denied by the crossbar.'

'And it's Sid,' screamed Harry the Substitute. 'He's seeking out Tracy. She's spotted the ball. She's let fly . . . it's a goal!'

The bench leapt in the air.

'West Oldfie-ld,' chanted the nine fans.

'Two–one!' whispered Chaz.

Suddenly there was a tiny chance they might not lose – and the team smelt it.

Vince took the ball down the wing. He dodged a defender but the ball went out of play. It was a Trafford Old Place throw. Gita intercepted and flicked it to Vince. He found Tracy. Then on to Sid. It was a great first touch. It was a great finish. The final whistle blew – two–all.

So every Sunday Dan prepared his little meringues. All the team, even Sid, gave orders for their favourite fillings but sometimes he surprised them with a new taste.

The last game of the season was an away fixture at East Village Lane FC. They were fourteenth in the league. Critics said they'd do better if their players stayed on the pitch. But EVil FC aimed for an average of three red cards per game. This was the critical match.

'If we win,' said Chaz, 'we'll be off the bottom. A dream come true.'

Dan had prepared two trays of meringues. He felt the

team needed that extra something. Pre-match . . . straw-berry and vanilla.

'What's for half-time?' asked Vince, his mouth full.

'Wait and see,' said Dan. He was feeling good. Even Sid was nice to him now. Other teams had heard about his secret recipe. Trafford Old Place had tried to poach him. They'd even promised him a game now and then. But Dan remained loyal to WORST FC.

Dastardly plans were being hatched in East Village Lane's changing room.

'Something's happened to West Oldfield,' said Virginia Jones. 'I think they're on atomic steroids.'

'Nah,' said Blades Wilkinson, 'it's them sweets.'

'I'm not being beaten by WORST FC,' snarled Erica the Red Card.

'I'll leave you to sort it,' said McThuggart the manager, with a horrible wink.

Erica the Red Card nobbled Vince with a sliding tackle. He limped off to the changing room. Erica got her red card and joined McThuggart on the bench, just as she'd planned.

'On you go, son.' Chaz pushed a reluctant Harry the Substitute forward. 'Remember, look for that loose ball – and try to keep your shorts up.'

Ten minutes before half-time, Dan was passed a note.

Ergent. Emergensy first Aid needed.

Bring sweets to the changing room. NOW!

~~Your sincearly~~

~~Yours Cloverely~~

from
Vince

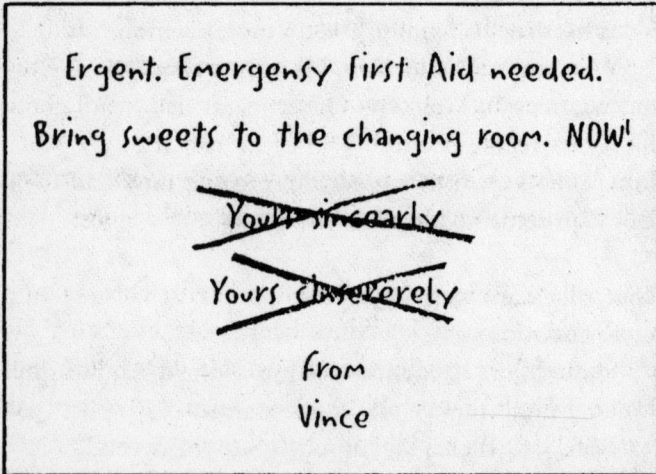

Dan rushed into the building.

Suddenly hands covered his eyes. Someone snatched his tray. He was pushed into a dark cupboard. He heard the key turn. He hammered at the door. He shouted, but everyone was on the pitch.

There was a small window high up. Dan climbed on the shelves and tried to squeeze through. He had to get his meringues back. The team depended on him.

'Where's Dan?' asked Sid at half-time.

'Where's my meringue?' asked Jim the Goalie.

Chaz Patel took charge. 'You'll be all right, you've had a pre-match sweet. Vince, go and find Dan.' Vince limped off. 'Now, Gita, watch out for Ginnie Jones. Let's defend deep. Let's play tight. We've held them to nil–nil. Just focus on that fourteenth place.'

Chaz was right. The match was the thing. But was one meringue going to be enough?

Dan was stuck. Stuck in the tiny window. He shouted and screamed. Surely someone would come along.

East Village Lane stuffed their faces with Dan's lemon sherbet meringues. Dan had been experimenting. He thought lemon sherbet might give the team more fizz. He was right. Every thirty seconds, an EViL FC player would clutch their belly and belch. Loudly.

'I feel as sick as a parrot,' groaned Ginnie Jones.

Tracy dazzled the burping defenders with her dribbling. She darted forwards and feinted to the right. She lofted the ball across to Sid, who had come fast down the wing. Sid volleyed it back to Tracy. She sprang into the air and headed the ball into the net. The seventeen WORST FC fans did a Mexican wave. Their team was one–nil up.

Ginnie Jones had had enough. When the ref wasn't looking she head-butted Tracy.

Chaz rushed on with Dan's sponge. 'How many fingers am I holding up?' he asked her anxiously.

'Half-past two,' said Tracy. She wandered off the pitch.

Stuck in his window Dan had heard the roar from the crowd. EViL FC must have scored. Then he saw Tracy tottering along.

'Tracy!' he shouted. 'Give us a hand.'

'Right at the lights,' said Tracy. She turned left and disappeared. Then Vince limped by.

'Hi, Dan,' he called. 'Seen Tracy? The ambulance is here.'

'She went that way . . . Hey, Vince!' But Vince had gone.

At last to his relief, Chaz ran up. He struggled to get Dan free.

'You didn't have to go into hiding,' he said. 'It's not that bad. We're one–nil up . . .'

'No,' began Dan. 'It was EViL FC. They . . .'

But Chaz wasn't listening. '. . . It's not that good either,' he continued. 'Tracy's off the field with concussion. I need you to play.'

Dan's dream was coming true. He was going to take to the field as a member of West Oldfield Road Sunday Team. And he could do it. He was goal-hungry.

Dan lumbered on to the pitch. He jogged up and down in his own half. He was about to do some press-ups when the ball rolled towards him. He was going to get his first touch! EViL FC were down to nine players but they looked like ninety as they advanced on him. Panicking he swung his foot hard and there was the ball, in the back of the net. His own net.

Suddenly the dark cupboard seemed like a good place to be.

Dan was angry. Angry with himself for messing up, and angry with EViL FC. He ran towards a hiccuping

Blades Wilkinson who had possession. Blades swayed to the left and thought he had sold Dan a dummy but found the ball had gone. Dan didn't know how he'd done it. He tried to pass to Harry the Substitute on his left. It reached Gita on his right.

''Ere we go,' sang the fans.

The defenders fell back, burping, to pack the goal area. They looked ugly – and their mood wasn't good either.

'Come on, team,' yelled Chaz. 'It's not over till it's over.'

Gita made a perfect through ball to Sid but he was boxed in. He back-heeled it to land at Dan's feet. Dan trapped the ball in the curve of his left foot. He steadied it and then blasted a shot at goal. It bounced off a defender. Corner! Harry the Substitute took it. He chipped the ball into the penalty area. Sid pounced. He hammered it towards the goal. It hit the goalkeeper, who was belching and hanging weakly from the goal-post. Dan ran forwards to get into the action but tripped over his own feet. *Thump!* He collided with something and hit the ground as the final whistle went.

He lifted his mud-stained face to see the whole team coming towards him. He had let them down. He'd had his sweets stolen and he'd scored an own goal. But Sid and Harry the Substitute were grinning. They dragged him to his feet. Jim the Goalie kissed him!

'That was some header,' said Gita.

'The goalie didn't stand a chance!' yelled Sid.

They tried to lift him on to their shoulders and collapsed in a heap. Vince's and Gita's dads started fighting with the elation of it all.

'Dan, Dan, the half-time man!' chanted the fans.

Dan suddenly realized he had scored the winning goal. WORST FC had begun to climb up the league.

On Monday, Sid Trump and his mate could be heard all over the school bus.

'Obviously, we was well made up.'

'Think Dan'll be in the team now?'

'Yeah. He may be slow but he's got a wicked head.'

Dan sat proudly at the back of the school bus.

TINA
by Neil Arksey

'It's a *team* game!' screamed Tina, charging, full tilt, into the penalty area. 'Pass it, pea-brain! *Pass!*'

The cross came very late and low. Cutting in front of two defenders, it hit the ground between Tina and the third. Tina spotted an opening; without slowing she swerved, got her foot to the ball and blasted with maximum impact.

The late tackle sent her sprawling.

Tarmac is unforgiving. Tina hit it hip-first, hard and fast, her hands, arm and elbow taking the rest of the impact. She slid, she scraped, she bumped – finally she came to a crumpled stop.

She lay still. As soon as she moved, she knew she would feel the hurt.

'Nice shot, Teen.'

'Wicked goal!'

'Yeah – cushdie!'

Grins and nods beamed down from the gathering faces.

'Sorry.' The defender held out his hand; his eyes said he meant it. 'No hard feelings?'

Tina let him pull her up. As she shook his hand, she went dizzy; she had to clutch at him to steady herself.

'Is she all right?' A woman with mini-dreads and a tracksuit pushed her way through the players. Tina had noticed her earlier, watching the game. 'You OK?' she asked.

Tina nodded. 'Nothing a few months in hospital can't fix.'

'Mental hospital!' added someone. Chuckling and patting her on the back, the others began to shuffle off.

Tina hobbled two steps and winced.

'Can I help?' said the woman.

Tina stared down at her ripped and blooded jeans. 'Any good at miracles?' she said.

Tina lived with her mum, in a small flat just across from the estate; it was three minutes' jog from Tidemarsh, the youth club with the tarmac pitch. This evening, however, she had been driven home, by an international soccer star, in her gleaming black BMW convertible.

No, it wasn't a dream, nor was it delirium brought on with the earlier spells of dizziness. Taking pity on Tina's leg injuries, Tidemarsh's new 'sports-worker' had given her a lift. Cruising through the estate, Hope Akinlami, twenty-four years old and capped seventeen times for England, had told Tina she planned to start a team; Tina, she said, had 'remarkable talent'!

Tina glanced at the kitchen clock: 7:48 – her mum always worked late, but was usually home by eight. She was a consultant; Tina didn't know what she did exactly, but it was something important. Hurrying the salad, she bunged the fish into the microwave and limped over to the sink.

She kicked the kitchen unit – hard. Her jeans were ruined! Trying to wash out the blood, when they were so badly ripped, had been pointless.

The latch on the front door made its familiar click.

Bundling the wet jeans into a plastic bag, Tina stuffed them under a cushion and sat.

Her mum stared at her.

'Nice day?' chirped Tina.

Her mum raised an eyebrow. 'Me jus' finish work – why you ask?' She spoke Jamaican only when she was excited, or in a filthy bad mood. She shot Tina another cold stare and kissed her teeth.

Tina fidgeted uncomfortably.

'Yuh ave some-ting feh tell me?'

It was useless trying to hide stuff; her mum could sense guilt straightaway. Immaculate in her suit and heels, arms folded, she towered over Tina.

'Well?' she said.

The microwave pinged.

Tina struggled to her feet. 'I twisted my ankle,' she explained, as she hobbled. 'It's nothing serious.'

'Tina, do I look like an idiot?' The Jamaican had gone; her mother's tone was cold.

Tina shook her head. 'No, Mum.'

'Where are your jeans?'

'I put tracksuit bottoms on,' Tina patted her leg, 'because . . .'

'Bring them.'

Tina squirmed. 'Now?'

Her mum nodded.

'I can't,' said Tina.

'*Bring them!*' she commanded.

Retrieving the bag from under the cushion, Tina handed it over.

Her mum's face darkened. 'Football . . .' she muttered, as she examined the rips and holes. 'I *knew* it! This is *football*, isn't it?'

Tina backed away.

Her mum advanced. 'Answer me,' she thundered. '*Isn't it?*'

Tina nodded.

'Well, this is the last straw,' said her mum.' 'This *cannot* happen again.'

'No, Mum.'

'You don't need to tell *me*, young lady – I'm telling *you*. It will not – there will be *no more football*.'

Tina stared.

'You must learn the cost and value of things. Your

glamorous football stars may be able to afford the earth; your mother, however, cannot. And, therefore – *neither can you.*'

Tina looked at her feet.

'No more school matches *and* no more games at Tidemarsh, do you understand me?'

'But Mum . . .'

'I want your *word* – you will cease to play in either.'

'But . . .'

'But *nothing.* It is high time I put my foot down. Football is a boy's game, it's a rough game and you are at the age where it starts becoming rougher.' Holding out the dripping jeans, her mum let them drop to the floor. 'I cannot have you always coming home with ripped kit and torn clothes, nor will I have you limping around dressed like a raggedy tramp. Now – give me your word and show me your leg.'

'See-ya.'

'Yeah, later.'

Pulling her hood up over her head, Tina gave a short nod as she headed for the changing-room door. Outside, she took a couple of deep breaths. The pavilion verandah, was crowded with mums and dads waiting to collect their offspring. This was going to be tricky.

'Nice one!'

A firm hand patted her on the back, then another; more voices murmured congratulations.

'Great game, son.'

'Excellent.'

Nodding acknowledgement, Tina kept her eyes down and hurried her way through. She crossed the car park. A car horn sounded; she ignored it. It sounded again, straightaway.

'*Yo!*'

That was for her! Tina spun around to see a BMW convertible purring towards her, Hope's familiar face beaming from the driver's side window. Tina nodded, putting a finger to her lips.

'Word travels fast,' said Hope.

'It had better not travel far,' said Tina.

'One of your mates told me you were playing,' said Hope. 'Come on, I'll give you a lift home.'

The wind rushed against her face; leaning back with her eyes shut, Tina tapped her feet to the music. They were a few miles up the road before Hope turned down the volume.

'So what was all *this* business?' she said, putting a finger to her lips. 'Was I making too much noise for such a nice area?'

'I was worried you might shout my name,' said Tina.

'And?'

'I was playing for Bradfields.'

'Bradfields?' repeated Hope. 'What! not the boys' club?'

'Yeah,' said Tina. '*As a boy!*'

Hope burst out laughing.

Tina kissed her teeth. 'You think *that's* funny. Listen — I had to *get changed* as a boy, with all the Bradfields mob! Talk about tricky situations . . . I didn't know where to look! I've never been so embarrassed in my life!'

Hope was laughing so much she had tears in her eyes. 'The things you get up to!' she gasped.

'Yeah, well — never *never* again!' said Tina.

'When I heard you were playing,' said Hope, 'I assumed it was for the school. I thought maybe your mum had changed her tune.'

'I wish!' said Tina.

It had been more than two months since her mum had informed the school that Tina would no longer be playing for the soccer team.

'I've got a few mates over at Bradfields,' said Tina. 'They know I can still pass for a boy so, when their striker rang in sick, they called me. Their coach was none the wiser.'

'And how was it?' asked Hope.

'What — the match?' said Tina.

'No, the *deceiving*,' said Hope.

Tina shrugged. 'All that "boys only" rubbish should have died out ages ago,' she said. 'I misled a few people — so what? I would have loved to have told them the truth, to have seen all those mums and dads find out a *girl* put four past their sons!'

'I didn't mean *that* deception,' said Hope.

'Oh . . .' Tina glanced over, sheepish. 'You mean, Mum?'

Hope nodded.

Tina sighed. 'It's been so hard not playing,' she said. 'It's really done my head in. I mean – I *live* for footie.'

'I couldn't do it,' said Hope.

'I had to stay away from Tidemarsh altogether,' said Tina. 'That was the only way I was going to keep my word to Mum.'

'I guessed that was why we hadn't seen you,' said Hope.

'I've still had to watch my mates playing at school, and all I could do was stand on the sidelines, practising my ball skills. I'm getting pretty amazing at one-touch though! And last week, just doing combinations: foot-foot, thigh-thigh, shoulder-shoulder, chest and all that, I kept the ball in the air *for over an hour!*'

'I'm glad to hear you've not been wasting your time,' said Hope. 'It's all excellent training.'

'Yeah! But for what?' said Tina. 'I don't get to *play*.'

'You decided it was OK to play for boys' clubs,' said Hope.

'Well, Mum did only say I couldn't play at Tidemarsh, or for school,' said Tina, 'but today was enough. I've had it with boys' teams.'

'How about a *girls'* team?' said Hope. 'Did your mum say anything about those?'

Tina shook her head.

'Good,' said Hope, grinning, 'because *that's* what I came to ask you about . . .'

Hope had the team training twice a week after school:

54

two hours on a floodlit pitch, the other side of the borough. They were struggling in a league.

Hope introduced Tina to the team – 'a natural-born striker'. A girl called Katie had been playing up front because they had no-one else, but she was only too happy to move out to the wing where she felt more at home. There was no ill-feeling.

The team were all in their teens – Tina was more than three years younger than any of them; she could pass for a boy, but not quite for a teenager. Resentment about her age was to be expected but, with Hope always around, it never amounted to more than the odd comment. During training, Tina worked flat-out to live up to Hope's description, but her real chance to prove herself was going to be a match.

Every day between training sessions, they were meant to practise. Most of the girls had taken to doing it with Hope, down at Tidemarsh, but because she'd given her word to her mum, Tina did all her practising at home, in the back yard.

Everything was looking good – the only problem was matches. They were played on Wednesday evenings, and sometimes even home games finished after eight. If Tina's mum was not to find out, Tina had to be back at the flat by, at the latest, seven-thirty. The best solution Hope could come up with was to let Tina play in home games, substituting her off at half-time.

Her first match got off to a slow start. In the opening minutes the opposition took a shot at goal. It was deflected for a corner, and from then on, under driving pressure from the other side, her own midfield fell back into defensive play; the ball wasn't getting pushed forward. The situation was madly frustrating – Tina wanted that ball so badly, the temptation was to run back and join the fracas. But Hope was watching like a hawk from the sidelines and, every time Tina drifted too far back, Hope yelled her forward.

At last, the longed-for pass arrived – more than ten minutes into the game. Turning on the ball, Tina tore up the field, making a bee-line for a point between two opposition defenders. The rest of the team were too far forward and, apart from two players and their goalie, nothing lay between her and the net.

As she sprinted with the ball, Tina checked first over one shoulder, then the other – with her freshness and speed, she had put a good fifteen metres between herself and the rest of the field. 'Go it alone!' yelled Hope, just as she was having that very thought.

She was going almost flat-out when the first defender tried to block her way. By the way the girl was moving, Tina could tell she was not only big, but clumsy. Pushing the ball through the girl's legs, Tina bounced off her hip, recovered her balance and carried on, hardly losing momentum.

The second defender came out a little more cautiously; she looked nimbler on her feet. Still a good ten metres off the penalty area, Tina slowed a little and veered sharply left, drawing the defender over to block.

It was now or never. Twisting sideways and accelerating across the pitch, Tina broke clear three metres, looked up one last time for a bearing on goalie and goal, then blasted the ball at the top right corner.

'*YEE-EAH-SSS!*' Tina found herself being crushed, as the girls crowded round to congratulate her. She laughed till she dropped, giddy with the thrill of the goal and overjoyed by the reaction of her teammates. Katie came over and pulled her up.

Five minutes later, Tina was taking another shot at goal. This time the goalie got to it and pushed it round the post, giving away a corner. Katie jogged over to take it. She boosted it high; the players in the goalmouth watched it float above their heads. But not Tina. Charging in, she took a soaring leap, got her head to the ball with a flick and put her second in the back of the net.

'*YEE-EAH-SSS!*'

The hat trick came just moments before half-time.

Dashing for the bus and home, her feelings were mixed – to have proved herself so spectacularly in the first game was wonderful, but then, having to abandon her teammates . . . Things could be better, but they had been a lot worse, she reminded herself. At least she was *playing*.

Tina wandered along the pavement eating crisps. The team had trained hard and finished early. Hope was giving her a lift home, so they could talk tactics before the cup final in two days time. Stopping off at a launderette, to put the team kit in for a wash, she had given Tina money for crisps and a drink.

Tina pushed open the door; the launderette was warm and busy. Hope was down at the far end, chatting to the woman doing the service wash. Tipping the tasty bits from the bottom of the packet into her mouth, Tina headed over. Hope was laughing. The woman turned. Tina froze. It was her *mum*!

Her mum stared. 'Tina?'

Tina stared back. She opened her mouth, but no words came out. Her mum stretched out a hand, as if she'd seen a ghost. Tina felt her jaw being pushed up, her mouth being closed.

'Chewed crisps and *saliva* . . .' said her mum, shaking her head. '*Not* a pretty sight.'

Hope looked from Tina to her mum and back again.

'This is my mum,' explained Tina. It was, but it wasn't. Mum was always smart and sophisticated. She'd never seen her look like this: hair up under some kind of shower-cap, and wearing an ugly, pale blue nylon workcoat.

Mum smiled coldly. 'Your friend here was just telling me about this young "star" of hers. She was saying how this girl has an excellent chance of an international career in women's football.' The smile dropped; her eyes became daggers. 'Surely she couldn't be talking about my *dis*respectful, *dis*honest, daughter?'

She turned slightly towards Hope. 'You've obviously

done very well for yourself,' she said. 'You have an expensive car and people recognize you in the street.'

Hope looked a little embarrassed.

'My daughter, as you must know, has always loved playing football, but, as her mother, a *single* mother, I have to think about her future. I don't want her neglecting her schoolwork. I don't want her finding, when she's older, she can only get a low-paid job.'

Hope nodded.

Her mum's eyes narrowed even further as she focused once again on Tina. 'But most importantly,' she said, her voice growing chilly and shrill, 'I do *not* want my daughter turning out to be a LIAR!'

In the silence that followed, Tina felt everyone in the launderette turn to look. 'I *didn't* break my word . . .' she suddenly blurted. 'I said I wouldn't play for school or Tidemarsh and *I haven't.*' She backed away. '*I* never lied . . .' she added, her voice growing louder, 'and I don't see why being a footballer can't be good enough for the daughter of a *WASHING CONSULTANT.*'

Tina felt the tumble-drier churning behind her.

Mum's eyes narrowed and her nostrils flared; she started to shake. 'You . . . you . . .'

Hope slipped between them, looking from Tina to her mum and back again. She smiled. 'A *washing consultant*?'

Tina's mum sneered. 'My daughter's idea of a joke.'

'It is not.'

'*Tina!*' her mum snapped. 'Do not contradict . . .'

'But you . . .'

'Enough!' Shaking her head, her mum turned to Hope. 'You see? *You see*? This is what I get – not one ounce of respect. A mother's reward – nothing but cheek and deception . . .' She wagged her finger at Hope. '. . . And *you* have had a part in this.'

Hope shrugged. 'I encouraged Tina to play football,' she said, 'if that's what you mean. It'd be a crime not to – she's very talented.'

Tina's mum humphed.

'She was very clear about what you had forbidden her to do,' continued Hope, 'and careful about keeping her word.'

Tina's mum kissed her teeth loudly. 'You *knew* I didn't want my daughter playing football . . . ?'

'Neither Tina nor I have set out to deceive you,' said Hope. 'If she no longer feels able to tell you what she's doing with her time, maybe some of the responsibility for that lies with you.' Hope turned to Tina. 'How come you didn't tell me your mum worked here?'

Tina opened her mouth to speak, but her mum got in first.

'Tina wouldn't have known . . .' she blurted. 'I often don't know myself . . . from day to day . . . the company owns a chain – I get moved around.'

'I had no idea,' said Tina, quietly shaking her head. 'Mum told me . . .'

'Listen!' her mum interrupted again. 'I know I've acted a little . . . I mean I shouldn't have shouted and I . . . I . . . the truth is . . .' She made a little choking sound.

'. . . The truth is . . . I wanted Tina to have something to *aspire* to . . .'

'I don't follow,' said Hope.

'Well, I . . . I didn't exactly tell Tina,' she coughed again, nodding in the direction of the washing-machines, 'I mean Tina didn't exactly know what it is I do for a living.'

'Mum, you . . .'

Her mum shot her a look.

'The truth is, Mum always told me she was a *consultant*,' said Tina.

Gripping a chair to steady herself, her mum sat down.

'Tina,' whispered Hope, 'give us a few minutes alone.'

The car door opened; grim-faced, Hope slid in behind the wheel. Tina lifted her head.

'You OK?' asked Hope.

Tina nodded. 'Is she angry?'

'Your mum says to say she's sorry . . .' said Hope. 'She was quite upset – I think it must have been really difficult for her, this whole thing happening at work and in front of her customers. It's not easy admitting you've told a lie – whatever the circumstances.'

Tina nodded and chewed her lip. 'I know.'

'But it's good to get things out in the open,' said Hope.

They stared at each other.

'I can't believe it,' said Tina. 'All these years she's been pretending . . .'

'She thought you might be ashamed; she wanted to give you something to aim for.' said Hope. 'Now the truth is out. She agreed with me – it's important to encourage and develop your natural talent . . .' A broad smile crept across Hope's face. . . . 'And so she's given permission for you to play the full match on Wednesday!'

'Yeah?' Tina grinned.

Hope nodded.

'Yeah!' shrieked Tina, punching the air.

'Your mum says, if she can get a few hours off, she's going to try and come along to the match.'

'Brilliant!' said Tina. 'I can't believe it!'

'It's true,' said Hope.

'At last,' said Tina.

'In the meantime, we'd better get you some rest.' Hope gave a friendly punch to her arm. 'Wednesday's going to be a *hard* game. Reckon you can cope with *two* halves?'

It had been as rough, tough and noisy a game as Tina had ever played. And a long one. It was 3–3, they were into injury time and everyone was *exhausted*.

'*Oi!*'

'Call for it!'

'*Watchit!!*'

The pass was as high as they come. With one eye on the soaring ball, Tina dodged sideways and backwards, bumping, pushing and jostling with the other players, for perfect positioning.

'Mine!' she yelled, launching herself skyward. A

last-minute shove from behind lost her the header, but she was still able to twist round mid-air and bring the ball down with her right foot. Trapping it, she skipped a scything tackle, swivelled 270° and took off into the other half.

Ahead: three players retreated, two came out to meet her. Tina slowed to a jog, looking over to right and left – nothing but opposition shirts. 'Come on!' she yelled, glancing behind. 'Where *are* you!' Feinting a swerve to the right, she pulled left, and nipped between the first two defenders. It was time to sprint again. 'Someone back me up!' she yelled, accelerating.

Over on her left, Katie exploded into view, pumping like a maniac, two metres clear of the nearest player. At last! Tina checked the three defenders up ahead, pushed the ball out a touch, whacked it and watched it curl across. Katie didn't even have to slow or deviate. 'Go with it!' yelled Tina, as the ball landed at her feet. And she did.

Confused defenders dithered between coming out to mark and falling back. Tina charged, full pelt, into the penalty area. From behind the goalmouth, she could hear her mother shouting for all she was worth. '*Gwaan* girl!' she yelled, as Katie's cross came floating over. '*Blaaast* it!'

Tina was inside the box and travelling like a rocket.

'We need this one!' bellowed Hope from the sidelines.

Tina dived. With her head, she cannoned the ball past the goalie, her whole body following through into the back of the net.

★

Hope and Tina walked, arm in arm, from the pavilion to the car park. The roof was down on the BMW and Tina's mum was sitting smiling in the back.

'Such a sweet picture,' said Hope. 'And such perfect timing – you landing at your mother's feet as the whistle blew.'

'She's really impressed by you,' said Tina, chuckling. 'She told me that when I start playing for England, she wants a car like yours!'

'Oh dear!' said Hope.

'It's all right,' said Tina. '*I* know women soccer players don't earn a lot, *and . . .*' she added, 'I know that's not your car.'

Hope stopped in her tracks. 'You do?'

Tina nodded. 'I saw the name in the log book when I was waiting outside the launderette.'

'My partner's,' said Hope. 'What did you tell your mum?'

Tina smiled. 'The truth, of course.'

'Which is?'

'Money and fame don't interest me,' laughed Tina. 'It's football I love.'

WINNING BY NUMBERS
by Dennis Whelehan

It was during the match against Bishop Chandler that Olly Brown first showed signs of strange behaviour.

Now, Olly looks odd – tall, thin, with a dreamy expression – and he's had crazy ideas for as long as I've known him. But he's never acted strangely before – at least, not during a match. And certainly not one as important as the quarter-finals of the County Schools Football Shield.

It was a cold, wet afternoon. There were few spectators – Barrow Road First XI had never won a trophy. Our sports master, Stoker Campbell, was there in his yellow cycling cape. He held up both hands – ten minutes to go. We were trailing one–nil.

We survived a corner, and our goalie saw the opening as quickly as I did.

'Quick, Tub,' I shouted, and started a run.

Tub Wilson rolled the ball. I was faster than the midfielder who came across to tackle me. I didn't try to beat him; I just kept running. Striped Bishop Chandler jerseys came streaming back. Ahead of them, taking long, ungainly strides, was Olly.

I took my eye off him and crossed the ball. I expected to see Olly's head ram it into the net. He was nowhere to be seen.

'Olly?' I shouted.

He was up at the halfway line. What was he doing there?

I had to get back because Bishop Chandler were attacking again. Tub may be shaped like a beach-ball, but he still managed to come streaking out of goal. He was raging mad because his motto is 'Leave nothing to chance'. He booted the ball clear.

Olly trapped it. Looking calmly around the field, he saw me. His pass was perfectly flighted. I hit it on the bounce. The Bishop Chandler goalie got a hand to it, but it skidded in. A lucky goal, but we were equal.

Then Bishop Chandler just threw the game away. One of their defenders wrestled Olly to the ground in the penalty area.

With penalties, Olly is deadly. I've never seen him miss. Olly hit it low, just inside the upright.

Barrow Road were in the semi-finals for the first time ever.

★

As we left the field, Stoker Campbell came over and joined us.

'What happened to you?' he said to Olly. 'You missed a sitter.'

He's called 'Stoker' because some kids claimed they saw him fighting under that name in a fairground boxing-booth. We put up with him because he really cares about football – without him, there wouldn't be any First XI.

Olly didn't answer right away. He was looking over his shoulder, studying the pitch as if he wanted to sketch it.

'I've been working on a maths project about tactics,' he said. 'It's called "Play Probability Theory", and it will win us the Shield.'

Stoker glared and did his chewing-broken-glass routine.

'Forget tactics,' said Stoker. 'Just keep sticking the ball in the onion-bag.'

I noticed some workmen unloading long poles from the back of a lorry in a corner of the playing field.

'Looks like they're making a new pitch,' I said.

Tub Wilson shook his head. 'Not likely in Barrow Road,' he said. 'There isn't enough interest in the game. And anyway, those poles are too long for goal posts.'

Stoker Campbell didn't even bother to look. All he said was, 'It's a sign of the times. And we won't be called "Barrow Road" much longer. The headmaster thinks we should have a more upmarket name.'

★

68

There was the usual messing about in the changing rooms. As team captain, I felt I had to do something before Stoker came charging in.

'Leave off,' I shouted as Olly's rucksack flew across the room. Then we caught sight of a framed picture.

'Who's the lucky girl?' Tub Wilson asked.

A roar of delight filled the room.

Olly blushed, and slowly drew out the picture. It was of Bobby Moore.

'Do you know who he was?' Olly asked reverently.

'Everybody on Earth knows that,' said Tub, 'including a few million Martians.'

Olly placed the picture carefully back into his rucksack. 'He was the supreme tactician, that's who he was.'

Tub and I exchanged glances. What was it this time? A special diet, to help strikers to jump higher? Hypnotism, to make the opposing team fall asleep? Meditation, to produce calm during goalmouth scrambles? Olly's crazes were always connected with football.

Later, as we were going home on the bus, Tub said, 'I wonder what old Stoker meant about "a sign of the times"?'

I didn't answer. The high we should have felt after winning a game was missing.

Which was very strange, because we didn't win all that many.

At the end of Assembly, the headmaster, Mr Rogers, asked to see the whole First XI in his office.

'He wants to congratulate us on reaching the semi-finals,' said Olly.

Tub carefully checked the contents of his pockets for incriminating evidence. 'Leave nothing to chance,' he said, quoting the goalie's motto.

Mr Rogers had been headmaster for less than a year. He had made many changes. Some were good – like speeding up the arrangements for school dinners and making people behave in the library. He said he wanted to give the school a new image – whatever that meant.

A light came on above the headmaster's door. We filed into his office and lined up before his desk – all fifteen of us, including reserves.

Mr Rogers was small and plump and wore a bow-tie. For a full minute he just sat and stared at us. Suddenly he pointed to a display-case on the far side of his office.

'Describe to me what you see in that case. You, Oliver Brown.'

Olly blushed. Day-dreaming, as usual. Probably about his football theory.

'Nothing, sir,' he stammered. 'It's empty.'

'Precisely,' said Mr Rogers. 'And it should be full. Full of cups and shields.'

We shuffled our feet.

'Not good enough,' said Mr Rogers. 'I have plans for this school, and they include success at sport. If we can't win trophies for one kind of football, then we'll have to try another.'

I could hardly believe my ears. I remembered the

workmen on the playing fields with the poles that were too long for goal posts – soccer goal posts! I remembered Stoker Campbell's comment – 'a sign of the times.'

Mr Rogers nodded as he counted the team.

'Fifteen,' he said. 'The exact number required. As from next season, if you lot don't win the County Schools Football Shield, this school will be playing rugby.' He gave one more nod to show that we were dismissed.

Stoker Campbell was waiting in the corridor. At first we were too stunned to speak.

'Is he serious?' gasped Tub.

'He's serious,' said Stoker grimly. 'There's the semis, and there's the final. Win both, or that's the end of soccer at Barrow Road.'

Olly acted almost normally during practice sessions. The presence of Stoker on the pitch saw to that. Olly performed the set pieces with his usual flair, happily whacking free kicks into the net.

It was during the five-a-side game that Olly's behaviour turned peculiar. During lulls in the game, he paced out sections of the pitch. He licked his finger and held it up to check wind direction. From time to time he made entries in his notebook.

When we were getting changed, Tub drew his attention to the framed picture of Bobby Moore.

'Still think he's the greatest?' he asked.

'The greatest tactician, yes,' said Olly precisely. 'He's the main reason why England won the World Cup in '66.'

Stoker was leaning against the doorpost, making sure everybody cleaned their boots before leaving. 'I can't agree with you there,' he said.

For once, Stoker spoke without growling. But Olly, a mild creature by nature, immediately boiled up.

'Have you seen Moore on videos? He always knows where the ball's going. That's tactics, that's genius.'

'I've seen him play,' replied Stoker, 'and I'm not taking anything away from him. But England won in '66 because the manager played Hurst instead of Greaves. I don't need to remind you that Hurst got a hat trick.'

Olly wanted to continue the argument, but Stoker was called away to terrorize some Year Fives. Olly grumbled all the way to the bus-stop. 'Look at some videos,' was the last thing he said to me before I jumped on the bus.

That evening I went to the paper-shop at the end of our street. It also rents videos. You have to be a member or over eighteen, but I used to deliver papers for Mr Rajaratnam, so he lets me borrow. I was looking for a sports video that featured Bobby Moore. The best I could get was the England–West Germany World Cup quarter-finals of 1970. We lost after a two–nil lead, but I still took it out.

I sat down to watch Bobby Moore. There was certainly something in Olly's claim. Moore popped up everywhere. His tackling was superb, but he won lots of balls by just anticipating passes. It was uncanny – he seemed to be in the right place at exactly the right time.

I put it all down to experience and skill, not tactics.

And certainly not some crazy theory.

But how could anyone convince Olly of that?

The semi-finals against Avon Bank began with a disaster. Olly sliced a back pass to Tub and let the Avon Bank winger in to score an easy goal. The point was that Olly shouldn't even have been playing in that part of the pitch. He was our top goal-scorer, for heaven's sake! We managed to hold the score like that until half-time.

I sat next to Tub while we drank our orange juice.

'You'll have to drop Olly for the final,' he said, mopping his face with his shirt. He knew that Stoker always consulted me when picking the team. Olly was sitting alone, turning pages in his notebook.

'Let's reach it first,' I said.

'You won't drop him because he's your best mate,' said Tub bitterly.

'That's not true,' I said. But it nearly was.

The second half was better. We stayed in the game because Tub threw himself around the goal, covering our mistakes.

Then I managed to release our winger, Billy Coleman, with a long pass. Was he offside? The Avon Bank defenders thought so. Billy drew the goalkeeper, then slipped the ball to Olly, who appeared from nowhere at his side. No error – one–all.

The cheers from our supporters were drowned by the howls of protest from Avon Bank.

The last thing we wanted was a replay, and the time

ticked away. And then came one of those freak accidents that decide a game. The Avon Bank captain, who had defended confidently until that moment, went up to clear a corner and headed past his own goalkeeper.

It was a rotten way to win. First a disputed goal, and now this. It should have spoiled our celebrations, but it didn't. After all, we were playing for a lot more than a football shield.

Tub nudged me in the ribs.

'Look at Olly,' he said.

Olly had spread a huge sheet of graph paper on a table in the maths room. He was carefully measuring and plotting with protractor and compass.

'That's the notorious maths project,' said Tub.

I leant across to read the title: *Play Probability in Areas of Accentuated Activity*.

'What does it mean?' I asked Tub.

'It means rugger next season, unless you drop him.'

That afternoon I waited for Olly after school. Usually he cycled home, but he pushed his bike and walked with me to the bus-stop.

'You've got to stop this nonsense, Olly,' I said. A stubborn look settled over his normally amiable face.

'It's applied trigonometry – perfectly logical. I've got a bit more data to find, then my theory is complete.'

I'm one of those people who has trouble counting his dinner-money, so I was already lost.

'What sort of data?' I asked.

'Angles of shooting and ball velocity, mostly. Oh, and a bit more about pitch utilization.'

He pulled a notebook out of his pocket and turned to a diagram of a football pitch. It was divided into squares shaded in different colours.

'It's quite simple,' he began, 'and absolutely foolproof.' A faraway look came into his eyes. He had forgotten me completely. 'You see,' he continued, 'in certain zones of a pitch there is accentuated activity – much more action, in other words. Now, if I could predict these—'

'Olly,' I interrupted, 'why not do what you do best – knocking in the goals?'

'This way is more scientific. It's about tactics really.' He patted his cycle-pannier approvingly.

'Have you got your picture of Bobby Moore in there?'

'I carry it everywhere,' he said.

'Bring it to the final,' I said. 'We'll need a lucky mascot.'

'It's got nothing to do with luck,' he said and, getting astride his bike, he waved goodbye.

Stoker Campbell sent for me the day before the final. We went into his office in the gym, and he made room for me to sit down amidst the clutter of sports gear.

'I'm picking the team for Saturday,' he said, scratching his cropped, grey head. He pointed to a list on his desk. Olly's name was underlined.

'You can guess the problem,' he said.

'Without Olly, we haven't a hope,' I said. 'So we really must play him.'

'He nearly lost us the last couple of games,' said Stoker.

'We had a talk,' I said. 'He had some loony idea about winning by numbers, but he's given all that up.'

'Glad to hear it,' said Stoker and ticked Olly's name. 'By the way, I hear those Kingswood lads can be a bit rough – both on and off the pitch.'

But I wasn't listening. After what I had just said, I had more to worry about than a hacked shin or a bit of stick from hostile supporters.

Tub and I were sharing a bench, lacing our boots, in the changing rooms of the sports centre where the final was being held. I was feeling nervous. It was our big day, and the situation wasn't helped by a visit from Mr Rogers just before we ran on to the field.

'You know how important this event is for Barrow Road,' he said, surveying us like a general inspecting his troops. 'And you know the consequences if we lose.'

Stoker Campbell, standing behind him, ground his teeth and gave a clenched-fist salute.

Olly was the only one unmoved by all this. He was smiling to himself and his lips moved as if he was making mathematical calculations.

'Looks chilly out there,' said Tub, pulling on a second jersey. 'Remember – leave nothing to chance.'

We had never played before such a crowd. As I ran to the centre circle to toss the coin, I felt nervous again. There was a lot of barracking from the Kingswood supporters and the Kingswood team looked like professional weight-lifters.

We won the toss, and I chose to play into the wind. We would save the advantage for the second half.

Kingswood were the present holders of the County Schools Football Shield. They had done their homework. Olly was tightly marked from the start. Not that it made much difference, since he spent most of the first half wandering from wing to wing. He had one solitary shot at goal. We conceded seven corners, and once again it was Tub who kept us in the game.

Our best chance came when the ref awarded us a free kick well up the field. I signalled to Olly and took it quickly. Olly began to run – but in the opposite direction! The ball trickled out for a goal kick. When Olly began racing up and down on a diagonal from the penalty spot to the edge of the halfway line, I could have hit him.

As we were leaving the field at half-time, with the score still nil—nil, Mr Rogers pushed his way through the spectators.

'Do you mind if I go, sir?' said Tub. He was dabbing his nose, which was dribbling blood from an encounter with one of the Kingswood strikers. Tub left with a spring in his step. The rest of us had to endure another of Mr Rogers' rousing speeches.

We were interrupted by Stoker Campbell.

'Something unpleasant has happened,' he said. He looked as if he was about to explode.

★

We stood and stared around the changing room. Our rucksacks and bags had been emptied on the floor and drenched with water. Benches were overturned, clothes strewn about. No need to look for the culprits. On the wall, in black marker, were the words 'Kingswood Rules'.

'It looks worse than it is,' said Stoker, who was making huge efforts to stay calm.

He spoke too soon.

We heard a shout, followed by a terrible cry of 'No!' Olly was kneeling on the floor, gathering up his picture of Bobby Moore. Both the glass and the frame were broken.

'It's only a mascot,' I said and tried to grab his arm, but he pulled away. He was in such a state that I was afraid he wouldn't be able to play out the second half. He flung the picture into a corner.

'Time to go, lads,' said Stoker Campbell.

Olly was first out. His face was white and his eyes were blazing.

We were prepared to put up with Olly drifting around the pitch for the whole of the second half: Olly on the wing, Olly in midfield, Olly anywhere but in front of the Kingswood goal.

What we weren't prepared for was Olly gone berserk. Far from drifting, he couldn't get enough of the ball. He chased everything and shouted constantly for passes.

'Cross it,' he yelled when I managed to get possession

a good twenty yards from the Kingswood goal.

'Move up,' I shouted back. A pass at that range would be wasted. Olly kept yelling and waving.

I overhit the pass. Olly kept running, then stretched his leg and met the ball on the volley. It flew, unstoppable, into the Kingswood goal. Olly ran into the net, grabbed the ball, and raced for the centre spot.

Kingswood tried to mark him out of the game. Olly just stretched his long legs and outpaced the defenders.

Kingswood tried to shut him out. They passed as soon as they got possession, they kept the ball on the grass, they barged, body-checked and swarmed whenever the ball came anywhere near Olly.

That didn't work either. Olly intercepted a duff clearance, played himself on-side, then streaked for goal. The goalie came out. Fatal. Two–nil.

Kingswood looked relieved when the whistle went. As it was, Olly made another goal for our winger, Billy Coleman, and we finished up with three.

Tub kept a clean sheet throughout.

Tub and I were on the bus going home. It was hours later and the celebrations were over. Soccer was safe at Barrow Road – for another season, at least.

I couldn't stop thinking about Olly.

'Amazing,' I said. 'After all, what was it but a broken picture? It could even have been broken by accident. Olly's such a calm character. It doesn't seem enough

provocation to make him junk his theory and start playing football.'

'That's what I was afraid of,' said Tub.

I shifted in my seat to get a better look at him. He
wore a self-satisfied smile on his plump cheeks.

'Meaning?' I said. I remembered that at half-time he
had left the field before the rest of us.

Tub reached into his bag and drew out the picture of
Bobby Moore. Somebody had carefully inked in one
front tooth and given him a moustache and an enormous
pair of spectacles.

'Goalie's motto,' said Tub with a grin. 'Remember?
Never leave anything to chance!'

HAVEN'T YOU FORGOTTEN
SOMETHING?

by Dennis Hamley

Danny was hanging about on the wing. So the others said. He, though, was seeing himself as Stanley Matthews – or Peter Harris of Portsmouth, who *would* be in the England team if the great Stanley wasn't so marvellous. If the ball came to either, he would set off in a mazy run, leaving the wing half and the full-back gasping, before putting in a pinpoint centre which would seem to hang in the air before Nat Lofthouse rose and nodded it into the net. Or Duggie Reid of Portsmouth.

Ah, now the ball *did* come to him, rolling along brown and shiny. Not a pass, though. It ran loose as Martin Downing and Ernie Styles clashed in a wild, leg-swinging tackle. So he set off on his mazy dribble. An airy wing half was left in his wake; an invisible full-back could only stare. He took the ball to where the goal line would be if Brazier's field boasted such a refinement, turned and hit it right-footed, aiming for that spot where the centre-forward's head would meet it before the goalie could cut it out. Except there was no centre-forward and the near post was a pile of coats. And there may as well be no centre-forward anyway. The ball skidded along the ground two metres behind the goal and Roger Hopkins stood accusingly, hands on hips.

'Daft twerp, Danny. Why can't you look what you're doing?' he shouted.

'He's too busy dreaming of Portsmouth,' Les Tofield sneered.

And why not? Most of the others came from families who had lived in the village for centuries. They all supported Arsenal, Spurs or even the Wolves, high up in the First Division. Danny must be the only Pompey supporter in the whole county. His family had only arrived in the village nine years ago, during the War, when Danny was three. He had inherited Portsmouth from his father – even though he had seen them only once, at Fratton Park, a day which stood like a jewel in his memory. A year and a half ago, September 10th 1949. A crowd of 41,000. Portsmouth, seven, Everton, nil.

But why not support the League champions, who were well on their way to a second championship and would have done the double last year if they hadn't unaccountably lost to second division Leicester City in the semi-final?

Jimmy Worth, tall and moon-faced, stood watching as he always did. The others wouldn't let him play. Only Danny seemed to feel guilty about watching him wait patiently for a kick at the ball.

At last Jimmy had a chance. He ran after it, picked it up and hoofed it back happily. 'There you are,' he shouted, as if expecting thanks.

The sun was going down. It would soon be too dark to play.

'I'm off,' somebody said. There was general agreement. Roger had picked the ball up.

'Here, have it back,' he said and neatly drop-kicked it to Danny. Well, it *was* his. If he didn't bring it, they couldn't play.

They all picked up their jackets, took off their boots, put their shoes on again and trailed off, Jimmy Worth following them. Danny was left holding the ball.

Ah well, it was Friday evening, no school tomorrow, so homework could wait until Sunday, along with Church. The *Hotspur* waited where he'd left it unopened to provide a treat when he returned. Another episode of *Cannonball Kidd*.

Cannonball Kidd. There was someone to envy. Centre-forward for Greyport Rovers, picked for England – *at the age of fourteen*. His only cloud – Mr Brasser was not only the manager of Greyport Rovers, he was Cannonball's form-teacher. But Cannonball always had the last laugh.

The last laugh. Something *he* never seemed to get.

Where had the others gone? Theirs might be a small village, but they all lived in different roads and his way took him home alone. They went to different schools too. Some were at the local secondary school. Others, like him, went to the grammar school six miles away. Yet others, exotically, caught the train to the big town and the technical school. If it wasn't for his football, the boys of the village might never all meet.

Soon he was home, reading *Cannonball Kidd* by the fire. As good as ever. Cannonball not only scored a hat trick against rivals Greyport Select, putting Rovers at the top of the league, but made Mr Brasser look stupid again – and discovered a great new centre-half playing on a local park.

Ah, what a life Cannonball had.

Danny stared into the fire, feeling he was missing out somehow. He thought of what it must be like to be Cannonball Kidd.

But the sight which kept on coming into his mind was not Cannonball cracking in the goals for Rovers and England, not Cannonball making Mr Brasser look a charlie again, but Cannonball just walking through a park and happening to spot that someone merely kicking a ball around with his mates would make a great centre-half. How had he done that?

I mean, thought Danny, could he have done it just strolling by our game tonight? Attack versus defence, six goals in, whoever was unlucky enough to be put in goal not liking it and tearing about all over the place leaving the goal undefended? Nobody ever played anywhere in particular.

Except him, out on the right wing. The only place where you *could* stand back and look . . . Well, could he do what Cannonball had done?

All right, let's try. Centre-half first. Someone calm, who could see what was going on, who could stop attackers and get their own attacks going. Someone who wouldn't get flustered.

Who, in their mad lot?

A large, sturdy figure came to mind, surprisingly fast, someone who could hit a ball first time and make it go more or less where he wanted it to, who could make anyone trying to get past him jar to a halt in full stride and wish they hadn't thought of it. Just like Reg Flewin of Pompey.

Pete Vaughan, that's who. He'd be a *great* centre-half.

Danny found a sheet of paper and a pencil. He drew out the time-honoured design – the way a football team played, which could never, ever change.

GOALKEEPER

RIGHT BACK   LEFT BACK

RIGHT HALF   CENTRE-HALF   LEFT HALF

OUTSIDE RIGHT INSIDE RIGHT   INSIDE LEFT OUTSIDE LEFT

CENTRE–FORWARD

He stared at it. Then he wrote, carefully, right in the

middle, below CENTRE-HALF, *Peter Vaughan*. Then, greatly daring, he wrote under OUTSIDE RIGHT his own name, *Danny Long*.

Two down. Nine to go. If anyone was a centre-forward, it was Les Tofield. Always hanging around the middle, sneering 'Rubbish' at anyone who shouted 'Offside', getting the ball between the coats anyhow – head, shoulders, knees, as well as with sudden savage shots which were sometimes on target and made Danny wince at the thought of a goalie trying to stop them.

Another name on the list. Who else? Martin Downing and Ernie Styles. Always tackling. Crushing collisions, tangling legs. Each other, mainly. Whoever won would hoof the ball far away, sometimes a mighty clearance, sometimes a chance for Jimmy Worth.

Full-backs – Martin Downing and Ernie Styles.

Half a team already. Two wing-halves, two inside-forwards and an outside-left to go. Very few left to choose from.

Outside-left – easy. Phil Carpenter tended to stay the other side of the field from Danny. The difference was – he was good. He ran like the wind – and remembered to take the ball with him. He could put over good crosses, or cut in and score on his own. Outside-left – Phil Carpenter.

Wing halves – difficult. Tough-tackling, thoughtful with it, able to set the forwards going. Pompey had the best. The two Jimmies, Scoular and Dickinson. He looked round his dwindling band for a Scoular and a Dickinson.

Wait. The Seaton twins, Mike and Reg. They looked alike, thought alike, played alike. They said little, but got on with things. They were always *there*. They *lived* like wing halves. Danny wrote them in.

Inside-right and inside-left now. You could have your second centre-forward, you could have your little fellow, your 'scheming inside-forward'. A tiny figure came to mind. He played neither for England nor Portsmouth, but the dreaded Arsenal. Jimmy Logie. Everything which went well for Arsenal started from this little man in the shirt and shorts which looked too big for him. Or Tommy Harmer of Spurs, gliding through defences like a ghost.

The second centre-forward was easy. Roger Hopkins, always trying to outdo Les, never quite making it.

There was one regular player at Brazier's field left. Midge Jackson had only one thing in common with Jimmy Logie. And with Tommy Harmer – he looked like a ghost. Could he scheme? Who could tell? He was always getting trampled on.

Size had to be qualification enough. In went the name.

Goalkeeper. Danny sighed. Who indeed?

His paper looked a mess. He took a clean sheet. He drew a line where the goalkeeper should be and wrote out the rest.

Martin Downing   Ernie Styles
Mike Seaton   Pete Vaughan   Reg Seaton
Danny Long   Roger Hopkins   Midge Jackson   Phil Carpenter
Les Tofield

That, thought Danny, would be a good team. The
trouble was, there weren't eleven others in the village for
it to play.

The clock on the mantelpiece struck eight. The wire-
less would be switched on now. The Light programme.
Take it From Here. Jimmy Edwards, Joy Nicholls and Dick
Bentley. His favourite show.

It rained the next day, though for early March it was
quite warm. Mum went on the bus to the town, shopping, and took Danny with her. In the afternoon, Dad
planted out potatoes and demanded Danny's help. By
five-thirty they were having kippers for tea and listening
to *Sports Report.* Pompey won again, two–one at home to
Burnley.

After tea, Danny put his boots and the ball into a bag
and wandered off to Brazier's field, wondering if anybody would be there.

Les, Roger and Midge were sitting on the wet grass.
They looked as if they had been waiting for him. Some
way off, Jimmy Worth stared with what seemed great
interest at the hedge, as if his being there was nothing to
do with them.

'You're lucky,' said Les. 'We were just going.'

Danny didn't answer. He sat on the ball and put his boots on. If the others were going, he noted, they'd have to take theirs off first.

Only four of them, though. Well, it was Saturday and the rest could have gone out for the day.

'There's not enough for a proper game,' said Roger.

'*He'll* have to play,' said Martin, indicating Jimmy Worth.

They looked at him.

'What's he got on his feet?' said Danny doubtfully. 'If they're big clodhoppers, he'll ruin my football.'

'Jimmy,' shouted Les. 'What's on your feet?'

Jimmy ran excitedly over. 'Plimsolls,' he cried.

'Don't you have football boots?' said Martin scornfully.

'Of course. But you lot never . . .'

The rest looked at each other and the beginnings of guilt at the unfinished sentence crossed their faces.

'We'll tread on your feet with our studs,' said Midge. 'You won't like that.' As studs had trodden over pretty well every part of him, he spoke with feeling.

'*I* don't care,' said Jimmy.

Danny received sudden inspiration. 'It wouldn't matter if you played in goal. We never have a proper goalie.'

'He'd be useless,' said Roger.

'He'd be out of the way though,' said Les.

So they played. Les and Danny versus Roger and Midge with Jimmy in goal: the winners to be the first to get six. Jimmy threw the ball out. Midge collected it.

Danny ran in to dispossess him. Midge flicked it away, saw Les run towards goal and away from Roger, lay back and hit the ball in a curling loop over Roger's head all of fifteen yards right into Les's path. Les steadied it and shot hard. The ball sped along the soft, wet grass towards the pile of coats, towards the corner. Jimmy jumped towards it, landed on his bottom and knocked the ball away with outstretched feet. Danny ran after it, reached it before Midge and hoofed it towards Roger, who shot with all his strength. Somehow, Jimmy scrambled up in time and was right behind it. He put his fists up in front of his face and beat it away. Midge this time beat Danny to the ball and got it back to Les, who tried to hit it first time. But he didn't time it right and the ball rose in a spinning arc high towards the goal. Jimmy was there again, looking as if he didn't quite know how to deal with this. Would he try to catch it, punch it, kick it? The others watched with bated breath. The answer came. He ran forward so the ball hit him on top of his head, rising high in the air and landing in the hedge.

'Goalkeepers don't do that,' said Roger critically.

'He's keeping it out, though,' said Les. 'I should have two by now.'

So it went on until dark descended, they picked up their coats and went home. They left behind them a sea of scarred mud, the ground cut up beneath their boots after the rain. But Midge had shown he *was* a scheming inside forward when he had space to avoid being trampled on. And Jimmy had kept the ball out somehow, anyhow. Winners first to get six? They hadn't put three past him all night. Ernie Butler of Portsmouth would have laughed his socks off at the sight.

Even so, as soon as he got home, Danny took out his sheet of paper and wrote 'Jimmy Worth' in that single blank space at the top of the page.

Danny was the only boy from the village in his class at school. Most of the rest came from the town. And half of them lived in an estate of new houses on the south side, called Baston Fields.

They all looked with scorn on the village people. This Monday was the same as ever. The winter game played by the boys at school was rugby. Danny knew nobody who liked it. He himself hated it. So playing proper football at home had a nicely subversive feel.

Of the Baston Fields lot, the two who got on Danny's nerves the most were Fulton and Spicer. You'd think, Danny often disgustedly mused to himself, that Baston Fields was like Beverley Hills. Well, it was all new and smart and the novelty couldn't have worn off yet.

Today they seemed very pleased with themselves. Danny soon knew why.

'We've formed our own football club,' said Spicer.

'Baston Villa. That's who we are,' said Fulton.

'We play on our new recreation ground. The pitch is marked out. And they've put goal posts up. That's what you get on a new estate.'

They didn't say, Danny noticed, who Baston Villa

actually *played*. And he *honestly* hadn't heard of them while he was making up his own team. But now he was goaded into saying it.

'I bet our team could beat you,' he said.

'*Your* team?' cried Fulton incredulously.

'What team's that, then?' said Spicer. 'Mangelworzels United?'

The team sheet was in his pocket. He took it out. They looked at it.

'Never heard of any of them. Except for Les and Martin,' said Spicer.

'It can't be much cop if *you're* in it,' said Fulton.

There was silence for a second or so. Then Fulton spoke. 'I bet if you came over to our place Saturday morning, kick-off ten o'clock, we'd knock hell out of you.'

'No chance. We'd win by three clear goals,' said Danny.

The bell rang. Mr Williams came in, loaded with books. Silence reigned.

They played in Brazier's field that evening. Midge got trampled on again. But, Danny realized, when he had some space to work in, he could be really good. And Jimmy, now with his boots on, flung himself all over the place like a demented spider. Legs, knees, feet, head – almost anything but his hands. But it seemed to work. Often Danny thought he could do pretty well in a real match – against Baston Villa or anybody else.

Before he went to sleep that night, a little voice at the back of his mind said, 'Haven't you forgotten something?'

He reviewed the day's events. 'No,' he said aloud. 'I don't think so.'

It rained on Tuesday. Wednesday was dull and Brazier's field was even more of a mess than it had been on Saturday. The game wasn't very enjoyable and Danny forgot all about his team. He got in a row when he arrived home and was shoved in the bath. The voice asking if he had forgotten something was not so loud that night.

On Thursday a letter came to all their homes. It was from Farmer Brazier. He'd found out they were playing on one of his fields without permission and from now on they'd have to find somewhere else.

Disaster. Their village was surrounded by wide green fields – but every one was owned by a farmer. Brazier's was the last they'd tried before being turned off. The recreation ground was about twenty yards square, with two swings and a slide. What could they do?

That night, the voice asking if he had forgotten something was squeezed out completely.

On Friday, Danny was preoccupied with their plight. He hardly heard a word all day. Fulton and Spicer kept looking at him strangely. He never noticed.

As the final bell rang and they all shambled out to go

home, Spicer grabbed him by the shoulder.

'All right for tomorrow then?' he hissed. It didn't sound a friendly enquiry.

'How come no-one in your lot knows about it?' Fulton, equally hostile, said.

'Knows about what?' stuttered Danny.

'Ten o'clock tomorrow. Your team plays Baston Villa. If not, come Monday, you're *dead*,' said Fulton.

'But that was only . . .' Danny couldn't find the words. 'We didn't *mean* it, did we?'

'Ten o'clock or you're *dead*,' Spicer repeated. They walked off together. Even from behind they looked threatening.

But he'd meant 'we *could*', not 'we *will*', hadn't he? He tried to remember Monday's conversation.

And then he remembered that voice in his mind. 'Haven't you forgotten something?'

Yes, he had. And it was too late now, with no Brazier's field to meet on.

His trudge to the bus seemed like the final walk down Death Row.

On the bus, Les and Martin looked just as intimidating. They usually sat well away, being a year ahead. This time they were right behind him.

'What's all this about?' said Les.

Danny tried to explain. 'I didn't think it was *real*,' he said. 'We didn't *mean* it.'

'You great twerp,' said Martin.

They sat back and left him alone. Danny hunched

forward miserably.

A moment later, there was a touch on his shoulder.

'Who's in the team then?' said Les.

Danny found his much-folded piece of paper and handed it over. They looked at it for some moments. Then Martin said, 'Not bad. That's quite sensible.'

Danny suddenly felt good. There was silence again except for the engine of the bus and chattering, screaming girls.

'We'll have to get round the village quickly,' said Les at last.

'They'll all be home now except the technical school lot,' said Martin.

'You'll have to go to the station and get them coming off the train,' said Les. 'That's your punishment.'

It wasn't much of a punishment. Before they got off the bus, Martin had thought up the idea of scrounging an old white shirt each and wearing school P.T. shorts. Then, after calling in home to let them know where he'd be, Danny ran off to the tiny station just as the hissing steam engine with its two coaches came in. Pete, Midge and the Seaton twins got off and slammed the doors behind them. Yes, they could all play. Yes they'd find white shirts and bring their school shorts. And, yes, they'd be at the church with their bikes at nine-fifteen tomorrow morning.

So would everyone Les and Martin found. Danny's paper team was actually going to *play*.

★

Next morning they rode the six miles to Baston Villa recreation ground. Half way there, Danny had a terrible thought. What if Fulton and Spicer were having *him* on and there was *no* team in red shirts waiting for them. Surely not?

They arrived. Yes, there were the Villa, waiting, kicking around, with Fulton's elder brother pledged to fairness as referee. They stared and Danny noted Fulton's look of slight surprise as the bicycles were thrown in a heap and Danny's team appeared, all in navy blue school shorts and white shirts, some short-sleeved, some with no collar, some with a faint stripe. But *nearly* all the same.

'We're like England,' said Midge proudly.

They kicked off. Danny felt he was in a dream. Last week a little fancy had come to him caused by a story about Cannonball Kidd – today IT WAS HAPPENING.

But there was no time to daydream. The game was swirling past all round him. From his position out on the right wing, Danny could watch – and wonder! Yes, his team really did play as their positions said they should. Pete *was* calmly breaking up Baston Villa attacks – and breaking centre-forward Spicer's heart. Martin and Ernie crunched into the opposing wingers and often got blown up for it. But they kept them out none the less. The Seaton twins in their quiet, determined way sought the ball and thought about how to use it. Les kept bundling his way forward, shooting whenever he could. Roger, a lankier version, did the same. Midge showed

98

what he could do before being clattered. Phil screamed down the left and managed some good crosses. First time out and they were playing like a *team*.

And what about Jimmy? He hurled himself about the goal. He kept the ball out with his feet, his shoulders, his knees. Once the ball was deflected over the bar off his right ear. Often the Baston forwards couldn't shoot for laughing. But they couldn't score either.

Danny didn't just spend his time looking either. It was his pass to Midge that got the goal just before half-time. In the instant before he was trampled on yet again, Midge managed to push the ball to Les. Les set off at the sort of rate which meant no-one was going to stop him and smashed the ball through the posts from six yards, leaving the Baston goalie wringing his hands and with a long run to make. The generosity of the local council didn't run to installing goal nets.

Baston Villa didn't like it. That wasn't supposed to happen. Throughout the second half they piled into the village goal. Everybody was back defending. Jimmy threw himself all over the place even more. It couldn't last. Ten minutes from time, Spicer managed a shot not even Jimmy could keep out, despite his long legs and bullet head. Now Baston went even harder for the winner.

Up to now, Fulton's elder brother had been a fair referee. But afterwards, Ernie swore blind this impartiality had left him. He didn't *deliberately* trip Fulton up in the penalty area. But the whistle blew – and there was less than a minute to go.

The village team stood mutinously as Spicer put the ball on the spot, eyed Jimmy with scorn, ran up and cracked it towards the corner.

Jimmy just smiled, took a huge leap across the goal, extended a long leg with its big boot on the end and cracked the ball first time up the pitch so that any village forward who hadn't been standing grumbling would have had a clear run for goal. Instead, they were mobbing Jimmy with their joy.

Too late anyway. The whistle blew. It was all over.

'Great game,' said Fulton. 'We'll do it again.'

'We'll come over to your place next time,' said Spicer.

Danny's team all looked at each other.

'You can't,' said Roger. 'The old farmer's taken our field off us.'

There was silence. Then Fulton's elder brother spoke.

'Don't you worry,' he said. 'When they know you put a team together and came all this way, someone will be shamed into finding you a pitch.'

Everyone felt very satisfied. A good game, an honourable draw – perhaps even, somebody muttered, the start of a league. Danny felt very proud.

Soon they left. They rode home slowly, contentedly, some with bruises and in pain they wouldn't tell anybody about.

Two miles from home, Jimmy of all people spoke.

'This was Danny's idea. He should have a reward.'

'Don't be stupid,' said Ernie. 'What reward can *we* give?'

But there *was* something Danny wanted. 'Thanks, Jimmy,' he said. 'About these white shirts . . .'

'What about them?' said Martin. 'Why shouldn't we look like England?'

'We could dye them,' said Danny.

'Any particular colour?' asked Pete.

'Don't tell me,' said Midge.

'I was thinking of blue,' said Danny. 'So they . . .'

'LOOK LIKE PORTSMOUTH,' everybody chorused.

But no-one said no.

SHOOT-OUT

by Paul Stewart

The score at full time was 2–2. A draw. But a draw was-
n't good enough, was it? Not for the championship. So
now we're in the middle of a penalty shoot-out to
decide who'll win the cup: Priory Middle or ST
JOSEPH'S!!!

We've had three attempts so far; they've had two. The
score is 1–1, and the atmosphere's mega-tense.

First Kev scored for us. Then Priory equalized. Then
Andy missed. Then their number four missed with a wild
shot that went way over the crossbar – thank heavens! –
followed by his boot. Then we missed again – or rather
John Read's shot was jammily saved. And now it's their
turn again.

It's funny how things turn out. If you'd asked me a week

ago what I thought I'd be doing now, I'd have said 'shopping'. That's what I usually do on a Saturday morning. Worse luck.

Sometimes, when Mum's in a specially good mood, she lets me off. Then I take my skateboard over the park. Or go swimming. Or go round Tommy's house . . . Whatever, I'd never have guessed that I'd be standing where I'm standing now – in between the goal posts and waiting for their number eight to shoot.

I've never felt so nervous in my life. Three more shots, Priory have got – and I've already chewed all my fingernails down to the skin.

I just wish it was over.

I mean, what am I doing here? I don't even *like* football!

No, that's not true. I love football. For a start, I support . . . well, a team. I'm not going to say who they are. But they're in the third division, and definitely on the up. Me, Dad and Grandad go to every home game. They first took me on my sixth birthday, and I haven't missed a match since.

They've got this brilliant new striker. Lee Perry. He's only eighteen. Five years older than me, and the highest scorer of the season.

Me? I'm not known for my scoring. Or tackling. Or dribbling. Or anything else really. But when I watch Perry streaking down towards the opponent's goal, it's me I see. Dummying, feinting, flicking the ball this way and that, past the sea of legs until – *kerpow!* – the ball

103

whistles over the goalie's outstretched fingers and into the net. 'YEAH!!' And I hang my head modestly as the rest of the team gather round, grinning and cheering and slapping me on the back . . .

If only!

Their number eight's taking his time. He's re-tying his boot-laces, making sure that he's completely prepared before his shot. He doesn't want to mess up like the number four.

I don't like it. It's giving me too much time to worry. My legs have gone all wobbly.

'Keep your eye on the ball,' I can hear my dad shouting from the sideline.

Shut up, Dad, I think. I know he's trying to help, but it's help I can do without. It reminds me that there are spectators. Loads of spectators. All ready to cheer – or jeer – whatever happens.

I look ahead. And there's Steve Tillin trying to get my attention. He points to the corner of the goal posts to my right. Then he grins and puts his thumbs up, encouraging me the way a good captain should.

Pity he isn't like that a bit more often.

Every dinner-time's the same. After our sandwiches, we all traipse over the field for a game of football.

'Let's pick sides,' says Howard Chapman. 'Me and Steve are captains.'

They always are. Steve, 'cause he's good – and

Howard, 'cause it's his ball. They toss to see who gets first choice, and then get down to the serious business of picking a winning team. John, Kev, Andy and Mickey always get snatched up first. They can all play well. Then come the so-so players. Those who are all right, but not brilliant. Ricky, Del, Alan, Ebby, Pete and Gal. One by one, they are all summoned, until there's just two left.

And it's always the same two. Lardy Clarke, and me.

No-one can remember where Lardy got his nickname. Some think it's 'cause of his posh lardy-da voice. Some think it's 'cause he's fat. Me, I think there's another reason. He's so pale, it looks as if his whole body's been moulded out of a gigantic blob of lard.

Being left till almost last is bad enough, but being lumped together with Lardy is just unfair. If everyone played like him, I'd be the Lee Perry of the team. Lardy's hopeless!

Unfortunately, that doesn't always stop him getting picked before me. The last two left always become the two goalies and, as Steve says, 'You're both useless, but Lardy fills up more of the goal.'

If he hadn't gone and got tonsilitis, it'd probably be Lardy in goal now. I wish it was.

I nod back at Steve, trying to look – what's the word? – nonchalant.

Yes, I think. Thumbs up for good luck, eh, Steve? And then it'll be 'Good Old Dave'. Unless the ball gets past me, of course. Then I'll be just a 'useless divet'!

I hate playing in a team. I hate the way everyone loves you one minute – and hates you the next.

The number eight has just finished double-knotting the lace of his second boot. He's stepping backwards, keeping his eyes fixed on the goal.

For an instant he looks up. I try to see where he's looking, but it's not clear. I remember what Steve told me.

'A goalie has three options in a penalty shoot-out,' he said. 'One, he can watch the run up to the ball and work out which way the ball's going to be kicked – the problem with this is that the striker will try to trick you. Two, he can commit himself to leaping left or right before the ball is kicked, and then stick with it. The problem with *this* is that if you choose the wrong way, you'll look a complete prat. And three . . .

The number eight has started trotting towards the ball. *Miss! Miss!* my head is screaming.

Closer to the ball, his right foot is pulled back . . . coming forwards . . .

He's going to kick it to my left. He is! I can see it. To the left! He boots the ball. I leap . . . suddenly I remember Steve pointing to the right. Something inside me hesitates. It's as though my body's turned to slow motion. Even as I stretch my fingers out to the ball – yes, it *has* come to the left – I know that that moment of doubt has made the difference between a glorious save and whoops of derision.

★

The score is two–one. I feel sick. My stomach is churning. To go the right way, to be so close and *still* to miss. It's so unfair!

I stare down at the ground, wishing it would swallow me up. If I keep on chewing the inside of my mouth, I'm going to end up with a hole in my cheek.

Suddenly a yell goes up. Is it the Priory lot cheering a miss? I look up. Pete's racing back from the goal, fists raised in triumph.

Two–all, and I was on again. Their captain was marching up towards the penalty spot. Uh-oh, my legs are turning to jelly again.

Of course, I was never meant to be playing. I was fifth reserve! But as the date of the Championship match got closer, I found myself rising up the list. First Ebby announced that his parents were taking him back to the Caribbean for a long holiday. Jammy so-'n-so. Then Del and Andy got this stomach bug from some iffy chicken. Then Patrick got knocked off his bike and sprained his wrist. And then . . . Yeah, well, Mickey had a spot of bad luck, too.

It was on Wednesday. We were all over the field as usual. I was on Steve's side and, for once, wasn't in goal. Reading his mind like a book, I raced up the outfield as John punted the ball ahead.

Controlling the ball brilliantly – Lee Perry, eat your heart out! – I sped towards the opposition goal. Lardy was off ill by this time, and Mickey was taking a turn as goalie.

As I streaked towards him, he never stood a chance. Though he tried. He came racing out from between the makeshift posts. But I was too good for him. I flicked the ball up and booted it, giving it everything I'd got.

At least, that's what I meant to do. But somehow, just as I'd got my right leg up, my left foot kind of slipped. Next thing I knew, neither foot was on the ground.

I was flying!

Then there was a crack and a thud, and I fell back and banged my head on the hard ground. But what about the ball? I twisted my head round, opened my eyes, and there it was – just dribbling between the two piles of sweatshirts.

I'd scored! I'd scored a goal. So why was no-one grinning and cheering and slapping me on the back.

'You divet!' I heard Howard saying. 'You useless divet!'

It was then that I noticed Mickey. He was writhing around on the ground, moaning.

'I'll go and tell someone,' said Gal, and sped off.

I'd broken Mickey's leg – his tibia. He had to stay in a cast for six months. Steve came up to me after the ambulance went.

'You'll have to play on Saturday,' he said. 'In goal.'

I didn't want to play at all. I specially didn't want to be in goal.

'Didn't you see me score just then?' I said, reliving my moment of glory.

'It was offside,' said Steve.

★

Their captain's placing the ball down. He scored both goals in the match – and now he's looking to make it a hat trick. He glances up at me and sneers. I chew my lip.

One, he can watch the run up to the ball, I think, trying to keep my mind occupied. Two, he can commit himself . . .

Blimey, he's coming! That was a bit sudden.

Before I even have time to think, I find myself going for option number two. I commit myself – to the left. It's a magnificent leap – piston legs, arched back, outstretched arms, grasping fingers. But is it the correct direction?

It is!

There's me, soaring through the air, and there's the ball hurtling towards the goal. Will they meet?

Yes, they will!

The ball lands with a slap. For a split second I feel the power of the shot forcing my hand back. But my body responds. It tenses and tightens, and pushes the ball away. And as the ball bounces off out of harm's way, I'm overwhelmed with a wave of goodwill from the team. It's incredible! Like being drenched in warm honey. Everyone thinks I'm magic! I hang my head modestly . . .

But then comes the inevitable question. What if you'd missed? I look up again. Even Steve Tillin's cheering. You didn't miss, did you? Misery-guts! You saved it. You foiled their best player. You've probably saved the match. YEAH!

And I did something I'd never done before. I punched the air.

So the score was still two–all. Steve soon made it three–two. Too soon! Here we go again, I realize, as their fifth player walks towards me for Priory's final shot at goal. It's their number nine. Even though their captain scored, it was the number nine who'd set up both goals with his spot-on passes. He's good. Very good. And from the swagger in his step I know he knows it, too.

The rest of the team go quiet. They – like me – understand that this is the most important kick of the game. If I save it, we win the cup – a first for St Joseph's. If not . . .

I don't feel good any more. Far from it. You're only as good as your last save, I remember, and shiver. I look from left to right. The goal posts seem to be miles apart. I watch the number nine placing the ball. He turns it round slowly until he's satisfied it's lying *exactly* where he wants it.

Slowly tucking his shirt into his shorts, he backs away thoughtfully. The teams don't matter any more. This isn't about Priory and St Joseph's. It isn't about the Cup. It's about him and me. The two of us. Two individuals trying to outwit the other. And I was going to win. For me! . . . not for the team.

It's impossible to tell where he's thinking of kicking the ball. Nothing registers on his face. Which is more than you could say for me. My cheeks are burning. My forehead's sweaty. I'm shaking.

I watch him breathe in slowly. He's preparing himself: mentally, physically. All at once, he's running towards the ball in measured strides. For the third time the goalie's options fill my head. One: watch the approach run. Two: commit yourself. Three . . . what *is* number three?

My hair feels itchy. My mouth is dry. I can't tell where he's going to put the ball – not a clue. But which way do I jump? I went to the left before, and it worked. Do I try the right this time? Or is that what he's expecting?

What's the third option? my head is screaming. What's number three?

Without looking up, number nine strikes the ball. A muffled *pock* echoed round the pitch. Everything else is silent. Everything else is still.

The ball leaves the ground and spins through the air, blurring the black and white hexagons. Watch. Commit. And . . . ? And . . . ?

I can't move. Not a muscle. My whole body's turned to rock. Wherever the ball's going, it's going there on its own. *I* wasn't going anywhere.

And yet! And yet! I can hardly believe it. A miracle is happening. The ball is coming to *me*! Straight towards my frozen body.

It lands with a thump against the tops of my legs. Instinctively, I double up and hug the ball to my body. I fall down on to the ground. And there I remain – still doubled up, still hugging – as every St Joseph's supporter goes wild.

Looking up, I see the rest of the team racing towards

me. They're grinning, they're cheering – the next moment they're slapping me on the back and hoisting me up on to their shoulders. And it feels *so* good!

'For me! . . . not for the team.' That's what I thought. But I was wrong. I was doing it for me *and* the team. It made the winning even better – eleven times better!

Suddenly, something Grandad is always saying comes back to me. 'The best player in the world is only as good as his team. Even your Lee Perry.' Yes, Grandad, I think, but only the best player gets carried off the pitch by the rest of the team.

And then I remember something else. I remember the third option. Number three: remain on the spot.

I grin to myself. Even being petrified can have its upside. I'll have to remember that next season.

THE B TEAM
by Narinder Dhami

'Go *on*, Jasmeen.' Kevin Jolly gave me an encouraging shove towards the classroom door. 'Go on. He's in there now. Go and ask him.'

'Yes, go and ask him, Jasmeen,' chorused the other members of the B team. 'Go on, go and ask him NOW.'

'All right, all right,' I said crossly, wishing I'd never had my brilliant idea in the first place. Or at least, that I hadn't opened my big mouth and told the others all about it. 'I said I'd go, and I will. Just give me a minute, OK?'

'You mean you're scared,' said Rebecca Lacey. Correctly, as it happened.

'Me? Scared of Mr Wilson?' I stuck my nose haughtily in the air. ''Course I'm not scared. Just watch me.'

I stalked over to the classroom door and flung it open, hoping that none of the kids in the corridor could hear my knees knocking against each other. I wasn't scared of Mr Wilson. Well, not much. No-one could really be scared of a teacher who had a face like a dopey basset-hound. But I *was* worried about what he'd say when I asked him what I was going to ask him. I'd never seen Mr Wilson get mad at anyone yet, but there was always a first time . . .

When Mr Wilson had turned up at our school last year claiming to be our new P.E. teacher, no-one had believed him at first. Mr Wilson wasn't big. He wasn't muscly. He didn't have a loud voice that nearly made you jump out of your skin. And he didn't make you almost faint with terror whenever he looked at you. Nope, Mr Wilson wasn't like a *real* P.E. teacher at all.

Mr Wilson was tall and thin and quiet. Weirdest of all, he was *kind*. He'd spend ages patiently showing you how to vault the horse or throw a ball straight or get over the high jump properly, telling you it didn't matter as long as you did your best. If you slid down the ropes in the gym too fast and burnt your hands, he didn't laugh his head off, like our old games teacher Mr Scott. And if you fell over in the playground and cut your knee, he always had a plaster in his pocket. He was kind and generous and nice. But, I asked myself, was he also daft enough to say yes to what I was about to ask him? Would he understand just how important this was to the B team?

There were about eight or nine of us in the B team. The school had its A team of course, the best players who played in all the football matches, and the B team kids were the ones who just hung around, hoping for a game. Anybody could be in the B team – all you had to do was like playing football, but not actually be very good at it. Still, although we weren't very good, we were keen. Most of the B team turned up for football practice on Tuesday nights most weeks, and Mr Wilson was very nice to us and gave us a ball to play with while he coached the A team. There was me, Jasmeen Sharma, who loved football but couldn't play to save my life; there was Tommy Grahame, whose mum didn't really like him playing football because she said he was delicate; there was Kevin, who was overweight, Rebecca, who wasn't bad, but just not quite good enough for the first team, and four or five others (a squint, a dodgy right leg and a couple of younger kids who were just plain rubbish).

All through the footie season we'd been hoping and hoping that at least one of us B-teamers would get a game, but none of us ever had. The first team had turned up for every match religiously, and we'd never been needed. We'd never even made it to the subs' bench. It wasn't fair. All the B team wanted to do was to play one lousy game.

Then I'd come up with my brilliant idea. Why didn't we ask Mr Wilson if the B team could play the last match of the season against Ferngate on Saturday? It would be a sort of reward for all those times we'd turned up to football practice and to the matches on Saturdays, and never even had a sniff of a proper game. Now all I had to do was to get Mr Wilson to agree . . .

'Yes, Jasmeen?' Mr Wilson was sitting at his desk, marking a pile of maths books. He looked up at me with those sad, basset-hound eyes. 'What can I do for you?'

I shuffled into the room, biting my lip. I'd spent the last hour deciding what I was going to say, and being coached by the rest of the B team, and I had it all worked out. But it still wasn't easy.

'Sir, you know it's the last game of the season on Saturday ...'

Mr Wilson nodded.

'And it really doesn't matter if we win or lose, because we aren't going to win the league anyway . . .'

'True.'

'And it's not a Cup match or anything—'

'Are you trying to rub in the fact that we haven't won anything this season, Jasmeen,' said Mr Wilson mildly, 'or are you getting to a point?'

'I'm getting to a point, sir.' I took a deep breath. 'We – that is, the B team – were wondering if *we* could play the last match of the season.'

There was silence for a few seconds. I suppose it was a bit much even for someone as kind and generous as Mr Wilson to take in. I mean, you just don't choose to play a team who can't even kick the ball straight, whatever the match is, do you?

'Well,' said Mr Wilson at last, 'I don't see why not . . .'

My jaw hit my chest. 'Really, sir? Do you mean it?'

'Of course I mean it,' Mr Wilson said firmly, almost as if he was trying to convince himself. 'I think it would be good for you all. Anyway, you deserve a chance, after coming to so many of the practices.'

'Thanks, sir!' I could hardly believe it had been that easy. We, the no-hopers, were really going to get a chance to play. 'There's only nine of us though, sir,' I reminded him breathlessly.

Mr Wilson looked thoughtful. 'Well, I'll put the two first team subs in, Joe Mills and Robin Chatterjee. They haven't had many games this season either.'

'Brilliant! Hey, you never know, sir,' I said eagerly, getting carried away by dreams of the B team suddenly becoming Premiership contenders, 'we might even win! I mean, it's only against Ferngate, and they've finished second to bottom in the league.'

Mr Wilson suddenly looked pained. 'No, Jasmeen, we're not playing Ferngate this Saturday. The fixtures had to be changed round completely when we had all that snow in January, remember?'

'Oh.' All my dreams of glory vanished in an instant. 'Who are we playing then?'

'Chipsdale.'

There was silence.

'Ch-Ch-Ch-Ch-Chipsdale?' I repeated weakly. Chipsdale. The Stormin' Normans of the Schools league. Thugs United. Their motto was: if you can't kick the ball, kick the other team instead.

Mr Wilson was looking at me anxiously. 'I knew I should have retyped that fixtures list,' he muttered. 'Perhaps it might be better if the first

118

team plays the match after all—'

'No,' I said feebly. I don't know why I wouldn't give in. After all, I was fond of my legs, and wanted to keep them roughly the same shape they were now. But it would just look so weak and pathetic if the B team didn't see this through. And it had been kind of Wilson to agree to let us play. I didn't want to throw that kindness back in his face. Anyway, if we pulled out now, we might never get another chance.

Mr Wilson looked like he was about to burst into tears. Then, suddenly, his face brightened. 'I'll tell you what I'll do,' he said eagerly. 'I'll have a word with Chipsdales' games teacher, Mr O'Brien, and see if I can persuade him to bring his second team over to play against you. How about that?'

I managed a weak grin. The chances of Mr Wilson persuading Nutter O'Brien to do anything were pretty microscopic. Mr O'Brien, the Incredible Hulk of Chipsdale School, was an old-style P.E. teacher extraordinaire.

'Thanks, sir.' I trudged over to the classroom door. 'I'll just go and tell the others the – er – good news.'

The rest of the B team pounced on me eagerly when I went back out into the corridor.

'Well?' Kevin Jolly grabbed my arm. 'What did he say?'

'He said yes,' I said cautiously.

'What, you mean we can play on Saturday?' Rebecca's eyes were round with excitement.

I nodded. I wasn't sure that there would be much

playing going on. More like rolling around in agony. I just hoped the school had plenty of stretchers and a hot-line to the local hospital.

'Y-E-E-S!' shouted Kevin and Tommy, and they conga-ed off down the corridor in delight, with the rest of the B team in hot pursuit.

I didn't say anything. It was only Monday today. The rest of the B team had four days until the match on Saturday before they needed to know that they were going to be in for the thrashing of their lives.

Approximately thirty minutes later the news that the B team were going to be playing Chipsdale on Saturday morning was all over the school like a rash. Silly me. I'd forgotten that the A team were going to be just very slightly peeved at not being able to play the last match of the season themselves; and they were spreading grue-some tales of Chipsdale's exploits with malicious glee.

'I couldn't walk for a week the last time we played Chipsdale,' said Leroy Browne, the first-team goalie, grinning all over his face. 'My leg swelled up like one of those long balloons.'

'I had to have four stitches in my head,' boasted Ricky Newman, the centre-forward. '*And* I had to have my foot X-rayed.'

Amanda Parker, who was the first team's only girl player, gave an exaggerated shudder. 'I'm really glad the first team aren't playing the match this Saturday,' she said smugly. 'I just can't stand the sight of that much blood.'

I glanced grimly at the other members of the B team, who were standing around listening in silence. Tommy Grahame was so white, he looked as if he was about to pass out.

'Right!' I yelled. 'Team meeting! Follow me.'

I hustled them all over to a quiet corner of the playground and fixed them with a steely glare.

'Don't *anybody* say they're not playing this Saturday,' I warned them in an icy tone. They all looked at me guiltily. 'What's it going to look like if we back out now?' I said angrily. 'We'll never hear the last of it.'

'But we're going to get *mashed*,' said Rebecca dolefully.

'OK, then we'll get mashed!' I said loudly. 'But we'll do it with our heads held high.'

'Not if we're rolling around on the pitch in agony, we won't,' muttered Kevin Jolly.

I glared at him. 'Wilson's trying to get O'Brien to bring Chipsdale's second team over for the match, anyway,' I said, trying to sound a whole lot more confident than I felt. No-one said anything, but they all had the same look on their faces – *no chance*.

'Well? *Does* anyone want to back out?' I asked coldly. No-one spoke. They all shuffled their feet, and looked glum. After they'd nagged and nagged me to ask Wilson if they could play, I suppose they felt a bit awkward about dropping out now.

The problem was, I was secretly wishing some of them *would* back out, so I could go back to Wilson and tell him it was all off, without losing face myself . . .

When we went back to class after playtime, Mr Wilson stopped me in the corridor.

'Oh, Jasmeen, I just phoned Chipsdale School, and had a word with Mr O'Brien.'

I stared hopefully up at Mr Wilson. But anybody could see by his face that it wasn't going to be good news.

'And it seems he isn't really that keen on bringing his second team over on Saturday . . .' That had to be the understatement of the century. I could just imagine O'Brien angrily roaring his head off down the phone line at poor old Mr Wilson for daring to suggest such a thing. 'So it looks like you'll be playing their first team after all.'

I gulped. 'Thanks for trying anyway, sir.'

Mr Wilson looked worried. 'I'll try speaking to Mr O'Brien again tomorrow.'

You've got more chance of persuading the sun not to shine, I thought sarcastically, but I didn't say so. I went gloomily into class, wondering if I'd still have the same number of limbs this time next week.

Like days always do when you're dreading something, Saturday came round at the speed of lightning. One minute it was Monday, the next it was Saturday morning, the match was twenty minutes away and I was sitting in the girls' cloakroom, putting on the school football strip.

'Red's never been my colour,' I said glumly to

Rebecca, standing up to look at myself in the red shirt and red and white shorts. 'Still, at least it won't show the blood.'

Rebecca gulped. 'I feel sick.'

'Don't try that old one.' I dragged her over to the door. 'Come on, let's get this over with.'

We went to meet the boys. They came trudging out of their cloakroom, looking like a bunch of no-hopers before we even hit the pitch. Even the two first-team subs looked as if they'd rather be somewhere a million miles away. The regular B team boys looked even more depressed. Kevin Jolly's football strip was too small, and Tommy Grahame's was too big. Side by side they looked like Laurel and Hardy.

'Ready, everyone?' I asked in a cheery voice that sounded horribly false, even to me. They all nodded silently, and the eleven of us walked slowly and gloomily down the corridor towards the playing field at the back of the school. All we needed now was an orchestra playing the *Funeral March*.

We got the biggest shock of our lives when we reached the football pitch. There was usually a handful of parents and kids who turned up to watch the game, but today there were what seemed like hundreds of people, all jostling for the best positions on the touchline. I scanned the crowd quickly. Most of the teachers were there, all of the first team and what looked like most of the town. I swallowed hard.

'They've come to see us get mashed,' said Rebecca Lacey faintly.

'This,' said Tommy Grahame in a trembling voice, 'is going to be the most terrible experience of my whole life.'

Mr Wilson came running over to us, looking like a string bean in a shiny green tracksuit, a whistle on a string bobbing round his neck.

'Chipsdale are a bit late, I'm afraid,' he said apologetically. 'I'm going back into school to wait for them. You lot have a kick-around to keep warm while you're waiting.' He threw the football he was carrying down on to the grass and it rolled towards Kevin Jolly. Kevin took a nervous kick at it, missed and skidded on a clump of muddy grass, landing heavily on one knee. A roar of approval went up from the crowd, and I groaned inwardly.

For the next five minutes we kicked the ball around between us in morose silence. I was just imagining happily that the Chipsdale minibus had been held up by armed robbers, Mr O'Brien had been taken hostage and the match had to be called off, when Mr Wilson waved at us from one of the windows.

'They're here,' he mouthed at us. 'They're just getting changed, and they'll be out in five minutes.'

A rustle of pleased anticipation ran through the crowd, and every member of the B team turned the same interesting shade of pale. Including me.

Five minutes later Mr O'Brien strode out of the school with a face like thunder. Chunky and massive in a bright blue tracksuit, he looked like the P.E. teacher from hell. Almost instinctively, the B team drew together in the middle of the pitch, shaking in our collective football boots.

The famous Chipsdale team of hard men was walking in a long line behind him. The goalie was first, wearing Chipsdale's green and black strip – and a pair of round glasses with thick lenses, held together in the middle by sticky tape. Marching along behind him were two boys who were smaller and weedier than my eight-year-old sister Sally, and behind them was a tall, thin boy who was bouncing a football up and down with one hand as he walked. At least he was trying to, but he was about as co-ordinated as Bambi on ice.

I didn't need to look at the rest of their team. A big grin split my face as I turned to the others.

'They've brought their B team! I don't know how Wilson did it, but he did it!'

Everyone, including me, sagged with utter relief.

'You mean we're not going to get mashed?' Rebecca squealed happily.

'Better than that,' I said in a determined voice. 'We can win this! Come on!'

'Did you see that bit where Chipsdale's goalie lost his glasses in the mud, and everyone was looking for them?'

'What about when Jasmeen's pony-tail got caught in that tall kid's braces?'

'That was awesome when Tommy's mum ran on and hit that Chipsdale defender with her umbrella.'

'And what about that goal Kevin Jolly scored? I've

never seen anyone score a goal with their *stomach* before . . .'

Everyone was saying there had never been a match quite like it. Even the A team had grudgingly admitted that. Yep, it had been a match to remember, for lots of reasons. Best of all, we'd won by four goals to three. It had been a close thing though. If that Chipsdale centre-forward hadn't tripped over his own boot-laces, they'd have equalized in the last minute.

'Four–three! Four–three! Four——three!' Aching, tired and muddy, but happy, the B team conga-ed its way down the corridor towards the cloakrooms, with me at the end of the line, holding on to Rebecca's waist. Mr Wilson was standing talking to some of the parents, but when he saw me waving at him, he came straight over.

'Well done, Jasmeen!' He clapped me on the back, and I winced. After I'd scored the first goal, Tommy had given me a congratulatory thump that had almost dislocated my shoulder. 'I knew you could do it.'

'Thanks to you, sir.' I lowered my voice and stared curiously at him. 'Sir, how on earth did you persuade Mr O'Brien to bring his B team?'

To my astonishment, old Wilson winked at me. 'Let's just say that I have great powers of persuasion, Jasmeen. Now run along and get changed.'

I don't know how he'd managed it. I wouldn't have thought anyone could persuade Nutter O'Brien to do anything he didn't want to do. But somehow Mr Wilson had. And one thing was for sure. Everyone now thought

Mr Wilson was the coolest P.E. teacher in the land.

Kevin Jolly came to school on Monday morning, and claimed that his dad had seen Mr Wilson and Mr O'Brien in The Green Dragon on the Friday night before the match. Kevin's dad said that they were having a best-of-three arm-wrestling contest, and that O'Brien had looked like thunder when he lost.

But we weren't quite sure whether to believe him or not.

PRESTON NORTH END
by Brian Morse

When Craig woke – 6:15 his bedside clock read – he was totally surprised to see a figure in a blue and white football strip sitting in the chair by his computer table. Craig peered through blurry, sleep-caked eyes at the apparition (the footballer, whoever it was, raised an eyebrow at him), decided he was having a rubbish dream and fell back to sleep.

When his alarm went at 7:45 and Mum called through his part open door, 'Time you were up, Craig!', the figure of the footballer was still there.

Craig sat up. 'Who let you in?' he asked. It wasn't the first question on his mind, just the first that came out.

The footballer stood up and smiled at Craig.

It occurred to Craig he had several choices. One was to shout, 'Mum! There's a strange footballer in my room!'

But somehow he didn't think that would bring Mum running. Another was to give a good old-fashioned scream – but then he had a feeling that wouldn't do much good either. By the time Mum arrived the figure would have disappeared. The fact was – and it didn't take many seconds to decide so – the figure was a ghost. It was unlikely to wait around for Mum. If it wanted to haunt him there wasn't much Craig could do.

'Well?' Craig asked, drawing the bedclothes tightly round him.

The footballer had an old-fashioned look. He had a thin moustache, his hair was short, particularly on the back and sides of his head and shiny with something greasy rubbed into it, and – this made Craig want to laugh (though he didn't do so out of politeness or in case the ghost turned out to be malignant) – the footballer's shorts were baggy and reached almost to his knees.

'Jim Grandison,' the apparition said. 'Preston North End, '31 to '39. Accrington Stanley and Newport County for a few years after the War. Free transfers. More than pleased to meet you but I won't shake hands.'

'Why not?' Craig said though not really wanting to know.

'The shock,' Jim said. 'Phant static they call it. Not fond of it myself. Plays havoc.' He shuddered. 'Look,' he went on, 'you can help me, Craig, old fellow.'

'How?' Craig asked.

'Your school's got a fixture in the Sandwell North Junior League this afternoon.'

130

'What?'

'Against Brick Kiln.'

'Yes,' Craig said feeling more and more that this was a crazy situation and it wouldn't be a bad idea to start the day again.

'You're playing,' Jim said.

'Of course. I'm captain.'

'I'm hoping you'll win.'

'So do I!' Craig said. 'Do you think we like losing?' (Said bitterly. They lost a lot!)

'Of course you don't,' Jim said. He looked Craig in the eye. 'I know this may seem strange to you but I've been watching you and your opponents. If we had a little chat you could be pretty certain you and your team would be more than happy with the results.'

'Watching us?' Craig said. 'Merry Hill? Why should you do that?'

'You'd be surprised how much interest there is in junior football on the astral professional football plane,' Jim said. Craig was, indeed, very surprised. Gobsmacked was the phrase that came to mind. 'As you can imagine, we ex-players have a fair bit of free time on our plates. So, we like to keep an eye on up-and-coming youngsters.'

'Up-and-coming youngsters? Us? Merry Hill?' Craig said, though he was thinking more of himself than of his teammates who were, frankly, pretty useless. 'Are we going to win the league then?' He laughed at his own joke.

Jim gave a ghostly shrug – which way to take it, Craig wasn't sure.

'Hey! You can't tell the future, can you? Take me for instance. Can you see me playing for Man United or England one day?'

Jim shook his head. 'That's a popular misconception about ghosts,' he said. 'I'm afraid the future's as much a blank to us as to you. Now, back to business.' The footballer spoke briskly. 'This afternoon's game. Would you like me to tell you something about your opponents, their strengths and weaknesses?'

'CRAIG!' Mum called up the stairs. 'Gone eight o'clock. You are going to be late.'

'Coming, Mum!' Craig turned to Jim. 'Brick Kiln – they're supposed to be pretty good. At least that's what our teacher Mr Nauta says.'

'Brick Kiln have their weak points, which you should be able to play on,' Jim said. 'I've studied their last half dozen games. Now what I suggest is—'

'CRAIG! ARE YOU COMING!' Mum bawled from the kitchen. The sound bounced around the stairwell, side-stepped into the bathroom then reached the bedroom.

'Hang on a moment,' Craig whispered to Jim. 'COMING! HONEST!' he called back. 'When you started you said I could help you. But it looks like it's the other way round. You're helping me.'

'You must have mis-heard me,' Jim said. 'I'm doing this solely from the goodness of my heart.'

'Don't trust him,' Craig thought. 'He's up to some-thing.'

Whatever his motives it was difficult not to feel grateful for Jim's information. It was spot on, invaluable, worth a couple of goals a game, minimum. And there was advice too about free kicks, throw-ins and footballing technique in general which Craig did his best to pass on to his teammates.

'We thrashed them,' Mr Nauta said in Assembly a couple of weeks later. 'That's three games on the trot we've won by massive margins. Brick Kiln Juniors, five–nil. Hallam, seven–one. Now Okker Hill, thirteen–nil. School – considering their inauspicious start to the season, your team have played like men inspired on their last three outings. Give them an enormous clap.'

'Old Nauta's going purple with excitement,' Gary, Craig's best friend, observed. 'You'd think it was him did the playing and not us.'

'Gary,' Craig whispered. 'Do you believe in ghosts?'

'Must be something in them,' Gary said. 'Clever people believe in them sometimes. Mind you, my gran believes in them. Cancel what I said.'

'What about footballers' ghosts?' Craig said. 'The great stadium in the sky?'

'You'd have a job to play football if all you are is a cloud of spirit,' Gary said. 'What's all these stupid ques-tions about? That's about the hundredth time you've mentioned ghosts in the last week. What's up with you?'

'Nothing,' Craig said indignantly. 'What does "in-auspicious" mean?'

'It means we lost the first four games without scoring a goal,' said Gary. 'I wonder sometimes why we're getting so brilliant.'

'Why don't you all make a Spooks super-league?' Craig asked next time Jim materialized in his bedroom.

'Watch my foot,' Jim said. He kicked an imaginary ball through the chest-of-drawers. His foot appeared on the other side. 'See.'

'You're never at the games,' Craig said. 'Where are you? Up in the sky, looking down?'

'I usually watch from the halfway line. It gives me the chance to see the play better.'

'I've never seen you there.'

'We don't try to draw attention to ourselves.'

'*We?*' Craig said. 'You mean there's lots of you?'

'There's usually a decent crowd,' Jim admitted. He was a bit reluctant. 'It helps of course though that we don't have to pay for entrance.'

'No-one does at school matches,' Craig pointed out.

'Of course not,' Jim said.

'I still don't get what's in it for you,' Craig said. 'I mean, if I was you I'd be out all over the world watch-ing the top class teams, not coming to watch us in Tipton.'

'That's the difference between people and ghosts,' Jim said. 'Ghosts learn to be less selfish.'

134

Nothing, Craig thought, would get him or anyone else nearly sane to watch Merry Hill on a wet winter afternoon. Unless there was something in it.

'I was pleased you took my advice about free kicks,' Jim Grandison said. 'Maybe we could think about crossing the ball. Your friend Gary could do with a little coaching.'

It was drizzling as they arrived at Hall Green for their next game. After they'd changed Mr Nauta made the team line up so he could give his pep talk.

'Make space,' Mr Nauta said. 'Gary, stick to your position on the right.'

Craig switched off. He thought of what Jim had told him – 'Hall Green's keeper's useless on his left. So always shoot to that side of him. The full-backs had an argument two weeks ago so the last thing they're going to do is help each other. There's a big lad with a loud voice. He looks really tough but actually he's scared of the ball and he hates falling over.'

Suddenly Craig wondered if Jim Grandison gave advice to other teams. And if not Jim Grandison, which other players from the great dressing room in the sky had teams under their wing? Did all teams have their minders?

Mr Nauta was finishing. 'Out there and give them hell!' he shouted.

Craig shivered. Was Jim Grandison from a footballer's heaven – or hell?

★

As they kicked off the sun came out momentarily and Craig noticed a man at the halfway line who looked suspiciously like Jim. Unnerved he shot to the right instead of the left of the goalkeeper. The goalkeeper produced the best save Craig had seen all season. '*We don't want to try to draw attention to ourselves*' – Craig remembered what Jim Grandison had said about the other ghostly spectators. He glanced around apprehensively. How many invisible figures were watching the game? Half a dozen? A dozen? Hundreds? Thousands?

Hall Green attacked down the right. Craig hardly noticed their supporters going wild as they scored. '*Easy Easy Easy!*' they chanted till the man on the halfway line turned out to be one of their teachers. He shut them up.

Play restarted. The big player who was scared of the ball picked the ball off Craig's toes, pushed the ball through Gary's legs, collected the ball on the other side of him and shot from twenty metres. The ball hit the crossbar. The big player put the rebound past Stephen, Merry Hill's goalkeeper.

Everyone was playing as badly as Craig. You wouldn't have thought they'd won the last game thirteen–nil and that Craig and Gary between them had scored eight of the goals. The defenders Jim had told Craig about were actually kicking each other as Craig, for only the second time, came within shooting distance. Even so, to take the ball off Craig, all one of the defenders had to do was accidentally stick out a foot as he punched his companion in the stomach.

Hall Green, five, Merry Hill, nil at half-time.

Mr Nauta was spitting with fury. 'You are letting the school down,' he hissed. 'I feel ashamed. Stephen – are you on their payroll? Gary – check which direction we're playing in when we start again. Craig – you are turning into a zombie. That can be the only explanation for the vague way you're wandering about the field. Merry Hill – you're worse than at the start of season!'

'Preston North End, sir?' Craig said suddenly. 'Who were they?'

'No time for a history lesson!' Mr Nauta snapped.

'History?'

'They were one of the teams that had to leave the league because they couldn't hack it! They weren't survivors! Nor will you lot be at this rate!'

'And Accrington Stanley and Newport County, sir?'

'More losers,' Mr Nauta snapped. 'What has this got to do with anything, boy?'

Craig wasn't sure if it had anything to do with anything but as he scored his sixth goal in seven minutes after the break he was sure he heard a ghostly wave of cheering from the bank of mist in the direction of the main road. Maybe what was happening was because Jim Grandison didn't want to spend all his life – or death, in this case – being a loser?

After Christmas, when Merry Hill had won ten games

on the trot and reached the head of Sandwell North Junior League, the local papers began to take an interest. LEAGUE UGLY DUCKLINGS TRANSFORMATION the *Echo* said. CRAIG CRACKS IN FORTY its rival, the *Post*, shouted. Craig had his picture in both papers.

Two games later Merry Hill were six points clear at the top of the league with only Parkside within reach. Craig had a look at the fixture list on Mr Nauta's notice-board. Merry Hill had four games to go, Parkside six. So Parkside had two games in hand. The last game of the season was going to be an exciting one for all concerned – Merry Hill versus Parkside. If both teams won their intervening games then whoever won the final game would be league champions.

Mr Nauta came up behind Craig.

'Sir,' Craig said. 'Parkside? Do you know how good they are?'

'As it happens,' Mr Nauta said, 'a friend coaches them. They had as bad a start to the season as us. I oughtn't tell you this, but I bet my friend a fiver that we would win the league. Craig,' he said, 'and please don't repeat this to anyone, but until you and the team began your unbroken run I wasn't the man to believe in miracles.'

Craig had a sudden vision of the sports teacher at Parkside saying exactly the same to his team captain. Also a vision of the team captain discussing tactics with his own player from the Hereafter.

'Sir,' he wanted to say to Mr Nauta, 'you don't believe in ghosts by any chance, do you?'

Of course he didn't say it.

He did, however, ask Jim the next time he materialized, 'What's there in it for you?'

Jim was sitting on top of Craig's wardrobe – he had a tendency to float off the computer chair when he was explaining tactics and, on the wardrobe with his head against the ceiling, their talks together were far easier.

Jim's reply reminded him of the one the footballer had made earlier – that ghosts were far less selfish.

'You and your team weren't enjoying your football before,' he said. 'Now you are. That gives me a great deal of satisfaction.'

'What about Parkside?' Craig said.

'Parkside?' Jim asked as if he hadn't heard of them.

'Who's coaching them, Jim?'

'Don't know what you're talking about, Craig.'

But Jim did know.

Uncle Mike was a Sheffield United supporter who travelled to see his team play whenever they were in the Midlands. Football didn't make him happy very often either.

'Jim Grandison?' he said. 'Twenty years before my time – longer, but I've heard his name. I think I've got him in one of my pre-War cigarette card collections. His main claim to fame was that he played for all three of the clubs that dropped out of the league – Preston North End, Accrington Stanley and Newport County – and he was the only player who did, ever. Fancy knowing wherever you went the club closed down behind you. Must have felt like being the kiss of death. There was something else about him, what was it? I just can't remember. Anyway, why should you ask about him? He must be dead by now!'

CLASH OF TITANS the headline in the *Echo* announced. Heading the two columns the paper gave to the coming game were pictures of Craig and the Parkside captain. The article compared the two teams' amazing records and the astounding similarities between their goal-scoring abilities.

Jim materialized as Craig looked at the article for the hundredth time.

'Last game,' he said. 'I don't think there's much more I can teach you.'

'You've been watching Parkside, I hope,' Craig said. 'Give us the low-down on them, then.' He put the article down.

'Parkside,' Jim said. 'Well, I was wondering – how shall I put it? Maybe it's a bit unfair you have insider knowledge all the time. After all it's only school football. Maybe other teams should have a chance.'

'Pardon?' Craig said.

'Maybe this is a game that should be decided on its merits,' Jim said. He didn't look at Craig directly.

'And Parkside aren't getting any advice about us?'

Jim didn't reply.

'This is a bit of a turn-about, isn't it? So you want

us to lose? Is that it?'

Jim looked up. From the look in his eyes Craig knew that was exactly what he wanted to happen: for Merry Hill to throw the game.

'You want me to fix the game? You can't mean it!'

The expression on Jim's face changed. He'd thought Craig was agreeing with him.

'Why do you want me to?'

'Listen,' Jim said. 'You owe me one. Without my help I doubt you'd have won a single game all season.'

'So we got good. Does that mean we have to give up right at the last moment?'

'You weren't supposed to win so many games. You weren't supposed to come top.' Jim got up and began pacing to and fro. 'My bet was that you'd come second. I didn't bet you'd come first.'

'You bet we were second best!' Craig said.

'You were hundredth best when you started,' said Jim.

'I asked about Jim Grandison,' Uncle Mike said that evening. 'He was a betting man. It was never ever proved but there was a suspicion he fixed a game now and then, missed an open goal on purpose. He was a forward, you know. His reputation followed him round. Not a very nice thing to be said about you, especially if it isn't true.'

Two press photographers were at the deciding game, together with about forty parents and most of the school.

'No tips about Parkside?' Gary said as they ran on the pitch. 'You usually have.'

'Not today,' Craig said. 'My source let me down.' He stared across at the Parkside captain – he recognized him from his newspaper photo. How he envied him all the little tips he'd got from his minder in the sky. Then he didn't envy him. Merry Hill under his captaincy could win this! He'd show Parkside which was the better team. He'd show Jim Grandison they were the best!

He called his team together.

'This is the way we're going to play it!' he said.

As they tossed he could tell from the way the Parkside captain looked at him that he knew all about Merry Hill's strengths and weaknesses. Craig thought – it must have been the way all the other team captains saw me looking at them!

We'll beat you! he vowed.

By half-time no-one had scored. Both sides had come close but either the shots had gone wide or the goal-keepers had made superhuman efforts to save.

Mr Nauta came trotting out with the drinks. For once he didn't offer any advice. Craig thought of the fiver Mr Nauta had on the outcome. Then he wondered what was at stake for Jim Grandison and his rival. He couldn't even begin to guess.

Then Parkside scored almost at the re-start from a simple lob down the centre which their captain collected.

It took ten minutes' hard work to get the equalizer and when it came Gary was the scorer.

One–all.

'Five minutes to go!' Mr Nauta yelled. 'Merry Hill – give it all you've got!'

Immediately Parkside were back on the attack. Craig felt as if his legs were made of lead and he knew from the desperate way that they defended that all the other Merry Hill players felt the same.

'Only a minute!' Mr Nauta said behind him as he took a throw-in.

'Give it straight back to me,' Craig said to Gary. He remembered from last week's article in the paper that Parkside were ahead on goal average. No use drawing.

Gary pushed the throw-in back to him. Craig took the ball up the left and pushed it back across to Gary. Gary went wide towards the right, beat one man, then another. He pulled the ball back across to Craig.

One person stood between him and the goalkeeper: the Parkside captain.

Craig hesitated.

The Parkside captain advanced on him.

With his left foot he hooked the ball over his opponent, then stepped past him and hammered the ball on the volley into the goal. The keeper didn't have a chance.

The whistle went for the goal, then for full time.

As Craig knelt on the ground, ready to raise his arms in victory he saw them. The astral footballers surrounded the pitch, tier after tier after tier of them, all on their feet and applauding him. He swivelled his head to look back towards the Merry Hill goal. There must have been tens of thousands of them.

He never saw Jim Grandison again. He sometimes imagined the phantom footballer apologizing for having tried to fix the game. He imagined him admitting Parkside versus Merry Hill had finally taught him football was all about the best team winning, not about winning bets. But Jim Grandison never came and, to tell the truth, Craig never had quite such a good season again, not even the one when he captained Man United to the treble. But very few people would believe that!

THE SPIDER KING
by Jonathan Kebbe

The school burned down the other night. Fingers are being pointed at me. I have an unfortunate record with fire: Mr Devito's corner-shop, Denny's golf-clubs, Pamela Johnson's hairdo. Now this.

I'm not a maniac, just a bit disturbed. I always carry a cigarette lighter. It makes me feel safe. Maybe I was a hunter in a previous life, saved from wild animals by fire.

I can see the school from my window, what's left of it. Until the fire, it was a neat collection of classrooms arranged around a high-ceilinged hall. Now it looks like Bosnia.

A police car draws up, my heart knocks with terror. Out climbs a meaty-looking copper in a leather jacket and a young policewoman in uniform. My mum, all trembly, lets them in.

'You again,' says the detective happily, like he knows I did it and isn't surprised.

My mother covers her mouth, too shocked to speak. We sit in the front room and I answer their questions gloomily. Mum chain-smokes and gazes desperately at me, like she can't believe her son's in such deep trouble, like she can't believe I'm her son.

'Not the first time, is it, Nick?' says the cop.

'What's not the first time?' I reply, avoiding the trap.

'Fond of fire, aren't we, Nick?'

I say nothing. I'm watching the clock, afraid Denny's going to come home from work, find the cops here and thrash me.

'Once tried to burn down Mr Devito's shop, didn't we?' says the cop, keeping up the pressure.

'He shouldn't have accused me of shop-lifting.'

'And set fire to Daddy's golf-bag, didn't we?'

'He's not my dad.'

'Lucky for you you're too young for prison. But you're not too young for a special school, where they send budding criminals and misfits.'

'Please don't take him away,' Mum pleads, wringing her hands.

The detective's staring at me. Calmly I return his gaze, quaking inside 'coz he scares me.

'You start fires when you're angry, don't you, Nick?' comes the kinder voice of the policewoman.

I think for a minute, but can't find a reply.

'What were you angry about this time, Nick?' she goes on.

Another trap. Same trap actually, different angle.

'You were booted off the team, weren't you, laddie?' taunts the detective. 'Banned from your beloved football for fighting in school. That got you all worked up, didn't it?'

My eyes start to sting. I fight back the tears as my mind drifts hopelessly. There's nothing left. Mum's tired of me, Denny hates me, most teachers are sick to death of me. Football's all I've got to keep me going. Before school, break-times, in the evening, wherever and whenever there's a pile of sweaters or a couple of rocks to make a goal, there you'll find me, blocking shots, plucking crosses from the air, hurling myself at players' feet.

'Spiderman' they call me, all arms and legs and madcap gymnastics.

Sometimes it's just me between the posts, alone against the world. Sometimes I'm Peter Schmeichel spreading myself high and wide to stop a hail of shots. Or I'm René Higuita of Columbia somersaulting through the air to save a certain goal in the daftest possible way, reducing everyone to helpless laughter.

Nothing gets past me. Well, not much. At least it wouldn't if our school had a half decent team. They lost eight–one today without me. Billy, my replacement, is willing but useless. It's like asking a clown to guard a bank. You have to be half mad to keep goal, but goal-keeping's a serious business and should be left to the professionals. In training I stand on my line with my back turned. The shooter shouts 'Ready?' and shoots, and I have to turn in time to see where it's going, and twist in mid-air if need be to make the save. Or I start out tucked up in the rigging of my net and swoop on the ball like snapping up a fly!

'Where were you between six and eight on Wednesday night?' the cop wants to know.

'Riding my bike.'

'You were seen near the school. What were you doing?'

'Riding around.'

'What time did you get home?'

'Oh, about seven,' Mum blurts out hopefully.

'Twenty-past,' I correct her.

'How do you know?' demands the cop.

'Rangers were playing Juventus.'

'You like Rangers?'

'I like Juventus.'

'We'd like to see his room,' says the detective.

Mum lets out a little gasp. 'It's not very tidy.'

They examine my room. They're up there ages. I don't know what they're after. Petrol? Dynamite? Uranium? They reappear with some cigarette lighters and my best goalie's gloves.

'Hey!' I protest. 'What are you doing with them?'

'They're going under the microscope, laddie. Be interesting to see what we find on them.'

Please hurry up and go! I silently plead with them,

glancing at the clock, terrified of Denny's return.

But they're not finished yet.

'The fire started in the headmaster's office, and he's the one who banned you from football, isn't he?'

I say nothing.

'You hate Mr Slim, don't you, Nick?'

'He hates me.'

'You told your mates you were going to get your own back on him, didn't you?'

'I was upset.'

The cop smiles. He's happy enough. 'That's all for now,' he tells my mum. Then he turns to me as they're leaving, 'But we'll be back again, I promise.'

They're gone. I breathe a sigh. My mum's crying. I go to comfort her but she shakes me off roughly, looking at me in horror, and I turn away stunned, meaning to climb to my room and hide, but someone's coming in the door and I freeze. I didn't hear him arrive.

'That was the police, wasn't it?' Denny's leaning over me, eyes blazing. 'It was you, wasn't it, you little . . .'

I back away from him and Mum tries to come between us, tries to tell him they found no evidence, but he pushes her aside and starts undoing his belt like they do in old films, all the time fixing me with his eyes.

Suddenly he flings out a hand to grab me but I'm too quick for him. I duck and swerve and leap the sofa in a single bound and strike out for the door . . . not knowing where on earth I'm going and wondering why Denny isn't running after me.

I know why when I reach the door. It's locked.

I spin round and there's Denny, shaking his head sadly as he comes towards me with the door key in one hand and his leather belt in the other.

Sometimes I wake in the night choking. In my dream I'm trying to reach my mum, who's trapped in a house-fire. She needs me, and I'm desperate to get to her. But I can never quite reach her; we always seem to miss in the smoke.

And all the time she's crying out in terror, there's a man in a flash car telling her to jump and he'll catch her. He doesn't look like Denny or Daddy, but I know it's one of them, come to save her. And I hate them, 'coz I wish it was me.

This time I wake up with my legs on fire, burning where Denny strapped me, and I lie here listening to the silence running through the house. I'll be tired in the morning, I'll fall asleep in school again and get in more trouble.

They've parked pre-fab classrooms in the playground while they're restoring the school. Everyone's eyes are on me – the firebug! Even my mates are strange with me. All this attention, I love it. Only it makes me lonely.

'Pyromaniac!' Pamela Johnson calls me.

'What's a pyromaniac?' I ask Miss Selby, my form teacher.

'Someone who can't help starting fires,' she replies. 'They're usually unhappy and need help.'

I don't need help – I think to myself – I just want things like they used to be before Mum and Dad started killing each other and Jenny left home in disgust.

She's all right is Miss Selby, the only teacher who ever smiled at my stupid behaviour in class. When she tells you off, it's soft and gentle like running water and you wish she was your mum.

'You got to talk to Mr Slim,' I tell her. 'He's no right banning me from playing. It's our last game.'

'He's got every right, Nick; he's the boss.'

'But he banned me for one game for fighting. Why is he banning me for another?'

'Because of what's happened.'

'It's not fair!'

'Shhh, not so loud,' she glances towards the door.

'They've nothing on me, nothing!'

'I tried talking to him, Nick, but while you're under investigation he won't have you representing Cherry Lane.'

'I thought you're supposed to be innocent till proved guilty.'

She studies me closely. The class watches in silence.

'I'll see what I can do,' she says.

Another night has passed and the police haven't been back, but that doesn't stop Denny going mad when he reads about me in the paper: BOY QUIZZED OVER SCHOOL INFERNO.

He swears at me for bringing shame on the family.

Family? I say. What family? And he tells me to watch my mouth, and I call him a rude name and he slaps my face so hard I run to my room and lock the door and crawl shaking into bed clutching a cigarette lighter, feeling like doing something crazy.

Next day, Miss Selby draws me aside.

'What happened?'

I say nothing.

She pushes the hair from my face to reveal a bruised eye. 'Who did this?'

I say nothing.

'Nick, look at me. Did this happen in school or outside?'

Still nothing.

'I don't suppose your stepfather – what's his name? Denny – had anything to do with it?'

'I'll smash his face,' I burst out. 'I'll run away and never come back and then they'll be sorry.'

'I don't think that would be such a good idea.'

'What do you know?' I snap. 'You were going to get me back in the team, remember?'

'I didn't say that.'

'You did!' I'm nearly yelling at her, afraid that even Miss Selby is going to give up on me.

'I said I'd do what I can.'

'So what are you doing?' I demand. 'Nothing, I bet. You're just going to let me rot while the team loses without me and I get sent to a special school.'

She goes white and looks out of the window. I've really upset her now.

'You don't care about me at all,' I shout, and I want to set fire to her desk. And I want to cry, 'coz I like her a lot and thought she liked me.

'I've made an appointment to see Mr Slim at four,' she says calmly. 'He said he was too busy to see me but I said it was extremely urgent.'

Embarrassed and ashamed, I twist up my face and scrunch my toes. Why am I always such a fool?

'Better watch out, miss,' I warn her. 'He'll eat you alive.'

'You think so?' she laughs nervously. 'We'll see.'

'Yeahhh!' I cry, shaking my fist triumphantly. 'Miss Selby's taking my case to the Supreme Court to get me off a murder rap!'

'Before you go, Nick . . .'

'What, miss?' I turn at the door.

'Come here, please.'

'What?'

'Look in my eyes.'

I can't.

'I said, look into my eyes.'

I obey.

'Did you do it?'

'Pardon?'

'I said, did you do it?'

I'm looking dizzily into her clear green eyes. 'No, miss.'

★

I hang around the shadows at lunch-time. Some of my mates invite me to play football, but I turn my back. I don't trust anyone any more.

Then I look away across the playground to the charred and twisted remains of the school and feel sick.

At four o'clock, I spy Miss Selby emerging from the Ladies Portakabin looking smartened up, with her hair tied back and the light of battle in her eyes. I tail her to Mr Slim's caravan, watch her knock nervously on the door and go in. I stand outside like I'm waiting to see Mr Slim, when really I want to listen.

As the argument hots up, I hear them going at each other like a married couple.

'Look out the window, Miss Selby; my school is in ruins.'

'But Mr Slim—'

'I've put half my life into this school—'

'But Mr Slim—'

'In ruins, Miss Selby, in ruins! Look at it!'

'But you don't know he did it.'

'Of course he did. He told everyone he was going to get his own back. Even if he didn't, I will not have that miscreant representing what's left of my school.'

Miscreant? What on earth's a miscreant?

'I don't consider Nick a miscreant, Headmaster.'

'Yes, well, that's typical of you, Miss Selby.'

'And what's that supposed to mean?'

'Defending the behaviour of rotten pupils.'

155

'Nick's not rotten.'

'Not rotten? Not rotten?!'

'A child's behaviour may sometimes be very bad indeed, but that doesn't make him or her bad.'

'That's quite enough, Miss Selby. I have a school to run and I don't have time to argue with staff who won't support me. So let me be perfectly clear. That boy is banned from the football team. When he's found guilty, as I'm sure he will be, I shall expel him, and he will be someone else's headache. Good afternoon, Miss Selby.'

Expecting Miss Selby to appear, I hop away from the door. When she doesn't, I lean closer once more.

'In that case, Headmaster,' I hear her say, 'you leave me no alternative but to resign.'

'You're not serious?'

'Nick assures me he's innocent and, until I learn otherwise, I have to believe him.'

'You're skating on thin ice, Miss Selby.'

'I'm sorry, Headmaster, but either Nick plays or I'm leaving.'

Silence. Not a sound from inside. Miss Selby must be standing there, patiently waiting Mr Slim's judgement.

Finally, 'I'll have to give it some thought, Miss Selby. I'll let you know tomorrow.'

When she steps out, I'm waiting to greet her with an excited thumbs-up.

'What are you doing?' she hisses, shaking me by the shoulders. 'Listening at keyholes, you little spy.'

156

She's all het up and furious, and I hate her and want to run. But she sees my rage and hurt and holds on to me.

'I'm sorry,' she says. 'It's OK.'

'It's because you think I'm guilty, isn't it?'

She looks me over again, and my heart beats sickeningly. 'I believe you,' she says. 'It's just that I don't want to lose my job.'

'He won't let you go,' I assure her.

'Want a bet?'

'We all like you too much, and so do our mums and dads.'

'I hope you're right, Nick.' She lightly touches my cheek with the back of her hand and I go red.

I'm sitting at the kitchen table trying to do some homework when the doorbell rings and I nearly jump out of my skin.

'Who can that be?' says Mum, looking out and seeing a strange car.

'Don't answer it, Mum,' I cry.

It's no use. She's opening the front door and goes, 'Oh, hello!' all flustered. Then I recognize the caller's voice – Miss Selby!

'I'm sorry to barge in on you like this. I should have phoned first.'

'That's all right,' says Mum, 'only if I'd known you were coming I'd have tidied up.'

What's she talking about? The place is like a museum.

Miss Selby's glowing. 'Good news,' she says. 'Mr Slim

says you can play.'

YES! I punch the air.

'And does that mean you're staying, miss?'

'Ah . . .' she frowns. 'That's the bad news.'

What! My heart sinks. 'You're not leaving, miss?'

'No,' she smiles, teasing me. 'He won't get rid of me that easily.'

YES! I punch the air again.

Mum makes a pot of tea. She's happy about Miss Selby but she's worried about me.

'I'm sure you would have heard from the police again,' Miss Selby reassures her, 'if Nick was still a prime suspect.'

It's funny seeing her sitting here sipping tea, like seeing someone stepping out of the TV into your front room. She's saying it's important I keep up my homework and football training, and that everything is as normal as possible. Then with a deep breath she adds, 'I'm rather concerned that someone's been hitting him.'

Mum's jaw drops, and right on cue Denny shuffles in from work. My mum makes the introductions. My teacher: my stepfather. Denny's all charm and smiles.

'I've heard so much about you, Miss Selby.'

'I've heard a bit about you,' Miss Selby replies.

'Nick's been given his place back on the team,' announces Mum.

'That's great news,' says Denny. 'Terrific!'

'Miss Selby says he must keep practising.'

'Naturally,' agrees Denny. 'I'm the one who's always

encouraging him – aren't I, Nick?'

'That's right,' I pipe up. 'He's always saying – For God's sake go out and play and give us a bit of peace.'

Denny goes red, gobsmacked. 'I thought you liked that shirt I got you?' he says.

I do. It's a beautiful black-and-gold goalie's top with the Champions League logo on the arm. He's not all bad, is Denny. He just hates me spending time with Mum. He wants her all to himself.

'I was also saying that someone's been hitting Nick,' says Miss Selby coolly, 'and I was wondering if you knew who might be responsible?'

Denny goes pale. 'What are you saying?' he jumps up, outraged.

'I'm merely asking,' my guardian angel smiles.

'You're accusing me, aren't you? Aren't you?'

'All I'm saying . . .' Miss Selby rises to leave, 'is that whoever is doing it had better stop.'

Saturday, grey and damp, the last match of the season. Cromer Park – arriving in a shiny white coach – need a single point to win the league. Our feeble little team is waiting on the pitch, needing a single point so as not to finish bottom.

Denny can't make it 'coz he's working. Mum said she'd come when she's finished her bits and pieces in town, so I expect she'll be along in a minute and join the other mums and dads who are shivering on the touchline and throwing me dark glances – Look! it's him, their faces say. The firebug!

I look away, mortified. And thrilled.

Mr Slim's showed up for a change, chatting stiffly to Cromer's fearsome-looking headmistress (a cross between Dracula and Mrs Thatcher). And there's a reporter from the *Gazette and* a photographer. Are they covering the match, or me?

I look around for Miss Selby, but there's no sign of her and I feel sad.

'How you feeling, Nick?'

It's old Mr Morgan, the teacher who runs the team, patting me nervously on the head like I'm an unpredictable dog.

Fine! I mean to say, but my mouth's too dry to speak.

'Where are your lucky gloves?' he asks.

My old worn gloves, my favourite gloves. The cops took them away. I always wear them, always! How can I save anything without them?

'I forgot them, sir.'

He lends me a pair belonging to the school. I try them on. They feel horrible, like dead skin.

'We need you on your very best form today, Nick,' he says. 'No acrobatics please.'

Acrobatics? Today? No chance. I've a bad feeling in my gut about today. I so want to do well, but I'm scared.

Usually, in a big match, I'm cool as Juve's Paulo Peruzzi, strutting around my goalmouth, lording it over my defenders. But now I'm all wobbly and twitchy, and I mess up from the start, fumbling crosses, mistiming my punches and failing to call for the ball. I'm scared of my teammates today, scared of the crowd and the hideous backdrop of the burned-out school. Scared of the ball. *SCARED!*

You need to be on sparkling form to keep Cromer out. They're a smoothly oiled machine led by two hot strikers and a beanpole centre-half who reminds me of boyhood photos of my dad . . . and soon the shots are raining down and I'm fighting for my life, leaping round my goal like a boy trapped in a house-fire.

What's happening? I'm thinking. This isn't me. I'm Mr Cool, not this fumbling nerd flapping about like a bird. And then the blow comes. A simple mis-hit shot looping towards me. I should catch it easily but somehow the ball slips through my fingers, and I'm watching it escape in slow motion, trickling over the line to nestle in the net.

Insults shouted from the touchline. I can't look.

Murmured groans from my teammates. I want to die.

One down and sinking fast. For the first time in Cherry Lane's history, we're going to finish bottom of the heap. Because of me.

It's a mystery how it's still one–nil at half-time. Luck rescues me time and again as Cromer whack my posts and bar and see their shots scrambled off the line by my bumbling defenders. Cromer are even denied a string of penalties by a ref who must be feeling sorry for us.

As he gives out the half-time oranges, Mr Morgan tears into me. 'What's wrong with you, you clumsy use-less bungling specimen of a goalie?' Actually he doesn't tear into me, but his eyes say it all, as do the eyes of everyone and I just want to bolt across the fields and into town and hide in the arcade and never show my face again. And I'm thinking, that's exactly what I'm going to do, run like hell, now!, when I feel these hands on me, and I stiffen with fright ... and relax, 'coz it's Miss Selby, working her fingers into my shoulders and talking softly. 'Calm down, Nick. You're a brave beautiful goalie, and no-one can take that away. Relax, and the magic will return . . . relax . . . relax . . .'

It almost works. When the game restarts I nearly find my feet again, nearly lose my terror. But I still can't blot out the crowd, the blackened school, Denny's angry face and my mother's cries in my dream, always out of reach. And moments later I really screw up.

Cromer's beanpole captain, the one who looks like my dad, bursts through our crumbling defence and instead of flinging myself on the ball I fling myself at him – at his throat! The look on his face! Half-strangled, half-hugged as I wrestle him to the ground and rub his face in the mud for good measure.

Well, what d'you think of that! my face says as I stand up and glare at everyone.

Any other ref would send me off – for ever! But this one must be the dad I never had, and all he does is smile regretfully and point at the penalty spot. My teammates turn away in disbelief. I hardly dare look towards the touchline, but this time I do, and what do I see? Mr Morgan instructing Billy 'Butterfingers' – our reserve

162

keeper – to warm up. He's taking me off! ME! the living spirit of René Higuita and Peter Schmeichel! The Golden Eagle of Goalies! Keeper of the Gates of Hell! Billy couldn't keep out a balloon. It's like replacing Batman with Mickey Mouse!

I'm so angry I could shred the ball with my teeth. Only the ref has hold of the ball and he's wiping the mud off (the cheek! Whose side is he on?) and placing it on the grubby spot.

And up steps Beanpole, all cool and cocky, measuring his run up. The nerve! Who does he think he is? Come on, Del Piero! Come on, Shearer! I'm ready for you.

He's ready too, pausing to contemplate the motionless ball, now raising his eyes to my goal, the wide open spaces either side of me. Does he dare look me in the eye? Does he hell. I'm me again, Lord of the Nets! I can read the minds of penalty-takers. I can *feel* which way they're going to go. It's in their knees, their hips, their eyes. You see there are three types of penalty-takers: the Trickster tries to send you the wrong way; the Bull decides which way he's going and sticks with it; and the Blind Bat just blazes. The Bat – strangely enough – is the hardest to read, because even he doesn't know where he's going.

This poncy prat is a trickster. I can see him kind of flirting with my left-hand post, trying to show me – That's where I'm going – when really he's planning the opposite. Unless of course he's double-bluffing, letting me see what he's thinking on purpose Complicated, but

not that complicated. Because there are two kinds of Tricksters: the cool ones; and those who just think they're cool. And Beanpole's one of *them*.

We'll soon see.

Here he comes, great lolloping strides up to the ball and wham! Good clean strike sounds sweet and flies true in a neat hard curve. But soon as he moves I'm airborne – please let it be in the right direction! me to my right and the ball to his left – and YES! the ball's under my body, trapped! – mine!

Beanpole wheels away in shame.

Applause lifts the sky.

I stand up grinning and salute the heavens with my fist. No modest in-betweens for me. I'm either dire . . . or the king!

I'm so happy and excited and free that I don't notice the police car turning off the road, creeping up behind the crowd, coming for me.

My penalty save inspires our raggle-taggle team. I can even afford to rest my pounding head against the cool of an upright, while at the far end of the field a concerted spell of pressure leads to a frantic, mud-flying shambles of a goal.

YEEOW! We've scored!

Delirium! 1–1. Little gutted Cherry Lane is level with mighty Cromer.

They're not amused. Minutes remain to score another, or they won't be champions, and they come at us like tigers out of a burning sky. But like dogs guarding a fresh carcase we hang on, back to back, fighting them off, me yelling encouragement and pulling off ridiculous, impossible, *outrageous* saves – bam! thud! thwack! Shots cannoning off my knees, elbows, any bit will do.

The whistle shrieks.

We've done it. We leap in the air and dance and hug. You'd think the Faeroe Islands had won the World Cup.

Mr Morgan's thumping me on the back, and Miss Selby is running up to plant a kiss on my brow, setting fire to my cheeks. Only Mr Slim isn't happy. As he's offering his commiserations to Cromer's Miss Dracula, he's looking strangely away. I follow his gaze and see the police car, and recognize the detective and the policewoman getting out and striding towards me.

I turn away and lose myself in the throng of players and spectators.

'Hey!' they call. 'Come back!'

I'm too quick for them. I duck down among the Portakabins and slip away round the stinking ruins of the school and run. If I'm quick enough, I'll get home in time to pack some things and find some cash and take off for the bus station.

Light is fading as I enter my street and pause to catch my breath. No sign of Mum, Denny or the police. Come on! I urge myself on. But I'm shaking so much I can barely throw one leg in front of the other. Come on, you fool, come on! Boy, Jenny's in for a surprise when I show up on her door. Hi, Sis, it's me! I'll write once a week to

Miss Selby, making her promise not to tell where I am.

I switch on lights and empty my kit bag and school bag on the floor, and stuff them with T-shirts, a sweater, best runners and a few favourite CDs. Then just as I'm rooting through Denny's things to nick my bus fare, I hear a car in the street and peer out. It's them!

The back door! Running downstairs, I scurry through the kitchen, heart hammering. Dropping my bags I fumble with the bolts and fling open the door and . . .

She's standing there, the policewoman, and I'm so startled I stumble back over my bags into the kitchen with the woman in blue coming after me, saying, 'Nick, it's all over.'

This frightens me even more and I run blindly through the house, too panicked to hear what she's saying.

'It's OK, we know it wasn't you. We've got the ones who did it.'

I stand frozen, gazing at her.

'Two older boys, out of their heads on drugs. They've confessed.'

She sits me down and goes to let her colleague in. He still frightens me, standing there in his mean leather jacket.

'I'm sorry,' he says, 'for giving you such a hard time. Here,' he takes something out of a bag. 'I threw away the lighters, but I got you these.'

Brand new goalie's gloves. Dead skin. Oh dear!

There's nothing left to say.

'We'll wait with you till your mum gets home,' offers the policewoman.

'It's OK. She'll be back in a minute.'

I stand at the window, gloves in hand, watching them drive away.

FOOTBALL FEVER

Collected by Tony Bradman

*Go for goal with these exciting and action-packed
soccer stories!*

Take a grandstand seat for some great soccer action: a
barefoot boy who beats the odds and amazes everyone
with his stunning skills; a goalie called Titch, who proves
height isn't everything when it comes to saving goals;
and the one and only Harry Jackson, determined to be
the best referee ever.

Tony Bradman has collected ten brand-new, action-
packed tales for this terrific collection of never-
before-published football stories from a team of top
children's authors including Rob Childs, Nick
Warburton and Geraldine McCaughrean. All the fun, the
drama, the action and excitement of the football field is
here, so kick off into the world of football fever!

0 552 529745

GOOD SPORTS!

A Bag of Sports Stories

Collected by Tony Bradman

Jump into this bag of sports stories and pull out hours of action-packed reading. Every one a winner!

Dive into the bag and meet . . . Dan, a talented swimmer who discovers an exhilarating new sport; Judith, who is determined to play in a tennis tournament; Sanjay and Michael, who run into trouble when they are picked to play for the school cricket team; and many other lively characters taking part in a variety of sports – from football and athletics to ice-skating, trampolining and skateboarding.

From a team of top children's authors including Robert Leeson, Michelle Magorian, Jean Ure, Jan Mark and Anthony Masters.

'A great read for sports-mad youngsters' THE JUNIOR BOOKSHELF

0 552 542962